SEX,

DRUGS,

BREAD ROLLS

&

ARMED
ROBBERIES

RIT

Editing, design, typesetting and publishing by UK Book Publishing

www.ukbookpublishing.com

ISBN: 978-1-915338-35-8

SEX, DRUGS, BREAD ROLLS & ARMED ROBBERIES

SEX, DRUGS, BREAD ROLLS & ARMED ROBBERIES

Let me tell you a story. I was a thirty-eight-year-old married mother of two the day I walked into the Store.

Until that day I had been working for myself across the length and breadth of England and Wales, up as far as Leeds, Manchester, Sheffield and Newcastle in the north, and down as far south as London. I really enjoyed the work, which consisted of running a promotions team both instore and across an extensive range of shopping malls and smaller stores. My team pushed a vast range of products to enable everyday living, if you needed it, and we demonstrated it alongside every new product that came onto the market. Or we ensured it was on the shelves of your local store, be it a massive Superstore or your corner shop.

Sadly, I had to give it up as the man I married was an insanely jealous control freak. They say love is blind, and in my case it was past the point where the relationship became abusive, it then became a cycle of abuse and his 'I am sorry it will not happen again' routine.

If I was late home for whatever reason, road accidents, traffic jams, I had, according to him, been with some man or other having sex in some car, hotel or lay-by. According to him there was no such thing as a traffic jam, or accident-causing traffic jams and backups – they just did not happen.

My husband would take the mileage of the car before I left home so he could check I "had not taken any detours to lovers' homes or hotels".

While I was out, he would check my undies drawer to see if there was any evidence to prove my I was being unfaithful, even only allowing me two sheets of loo paper on each bathroom visit – that is just a taster of what he was like to try and live with.

It got so bad I had to give up a very lucrative job to keep the peace, or so I thought.

The store was one in a national chain of a well-known company, which portrayed a wholesome family image. The money was poor but regular – at that time it came second to what I thought was going to bring some peace and calm to my troubled marriage.

My childhood had been horrendous. I was the eldest of four children born into a pit family just after the Second World War.

My grandfather came to our city from the Welsh mining valleys to work the local pit; he had cycled from the Rhonda Valley, sleeping in hedgerows on his way here to secure a job in the local colliery.

My mother was one of his five children, the only girl. In those days boys were all, so she being the only girl made her the brunt of all Granddad's anger issues.

Which, because I was her eldest child, she subsequently passed all those anger issues onto me – I was her whipping post and unpaid slave.

My siblings and I were locked in our bedroom at night, not even being allowed out to the toilet – we had to use a potty in the bedroom. If for some reason there was a problem at night in the room I shared with my two sisters both younger than me – her son being the apple of her eye was allowed to share our parents' bedroom even though there was a spare bedroom he could have used – she would send Dad up with a length of bamboo to thrash us with. We dared not make a sound at night in that room.

I lost count of the number of times I would be dragged out of bed by my mother in the middle of the night to go and persuade Dad to come back into the house from wherever he had gone to try and sleep, to escape my mother's nagging and vitriolic tirades, no matter what the weather. Be it the garden shed or in later years the cab of his lorry after he had left the pit when he had his accident at work.

It got so bad I started sleeping in my clothes, which caused its own problems as I became the girls at school's whipping post, called smelly and various other names.

All the stress I was under daily caused me to wet the bed until I was a teenager. I would dream I was sitting on the loo, and it was ok to urinate, when in fact I was still in my bed.

Not only were the nights horrific, my days were not much better. I was my mother's slave. Right from the age of five my earliest memories consisted of my mother making me cook breakfast for my siblings before going to school while she lovingly interacted with my brother, her star child. When she saw me watching her love and care for her special son, she smiled at me, walked over to me and punched me straight in the stomach so hard I couldn't breathe then just carried on walking.

If we had to be at my Grandparents' for any reason, I would go out of my way to help my Nan who I adored – she was kind and loving to me, so much so she asked my mum if I could go live with her and Granddad.

My mum was having none of that – she would have lost her slave.

When my mum came to pick us up from Nan's, we would all run to her for a hug. I never got one; I would always get a clip around the ear instead. It got to the stage where I could judge from the look in my mother's eye when the blow was about to be delivered, then time my duck to avoid it landing.

That would infuriate her even more; she would berate me, saying, "I will get you. I will come up the other way and catch you out."

This was my daily life. It did not matter what I did, I was my mother's punching bag, being dragged out of bed on a bright sunny morning, punched and shoved while she screamed at me to run after the tally man as he had missed our house.

I was half asleep, dazed and confused from the beating, when I caught up with the tally man. Between my sobbed explanation as to why I was chasing him up the street in just my knickers, he calmly and kindly told me to tell my mother he had not been down that side of the street yet, to stop crying and go home.

Upon my return to Mother after telling her what the tally man had said, I got another clip round the ear and told to get on with making my siblings breakfast.

In those days rationing was still about, so Mum kept chickens whose eggs she sold to the neighbours. At Christmas and Easter she would cull the older birds in the most barbaric way by placing a rolling pin across the bird's neck, then forcibly pulling its head from its neck. Mum all over – brutal.

Mum also kept pigeons and rabbits; they were our food. We all had a pet rabbit but nothing was safe – you learned not to get attached.

I will never forget the look on my brother's face the day he asked Mum where his pet rabbit was. Mum flippantly replied "in the oven". That is why my siblings and I never got attached to any pet – if you did it would be killed, just another way of torturing us all, but me especially.

I remember the day Granddad passed away. He had been sick for a long time with Miner's disease or Silicosis; we all knew he was sick, but did not realise he was terminal.

Mum came into the lounge and told Dad she was going over to see Granddad. I asked if I could go with her, but she said no and off she went. I needed the loo so went upstairs then into my bedroom as I usually did to gaze out of my window, from where I saw two men carrying a coffin out of Granddad's house to a hearse. I knew straight away Granddad was gone. I was in shock.

Mum saw me at my window and flew across the street. I could tell from her face she was as mad as hell. I stumbled downstairs to Dad, but as I got to the bottom of the stairs Mum erupted through the door, and rounded on me, punching and kicking me all the while screaming at Dad as to why he had not kept me downstairs.

No cuddle or hugs of consolation for losing my Granddad, just pure hate.

At age ten I started my periods, waking one morning covered in blood. I thought I was dying.

Mum's response was to give me a sanitary garment to put on which she had to show me how to use, telling me to get to school and to keep away from boys. I spent the whole day in abject misery thinking I'm dying and no one cares. When I got home Mum took me to the Doctor's, as I lay on the examination table with the doctor on one side and Mum on the other with the doctor asking Mum how old (she had been) her reply: seventeen years old. Our doctor told us to go home, still with no explanation as to what was wrong with me. On the way home Mum told me I was to wear a pad every day and to keep away from boys.

I started crying, which resulted in a clip around the ear from my mum, and getting told to shut up. I was terrified I was about to die and not a single soul cared. Until Gran came a couple of days later, she took one look at my face and asked me what was wrong. I burst into tears, informing her I was bleeding to death. Gran hugged me, proceeding to explain matters to me in a simple, loving way.

No matter to Mum I'd spent a week in abject terror and misery when if like Gran she could have just told me calmly what was happening – just another way for her to terrorise me.

So, in effect my life was a continuation of my mother's life. I thought I had married for love but with hindsight by marrying the man I did I had exchanged my mother for her male counterpart in my husband, with the same physical, and emotional abuse, and now sexual abuse also.

By giving up my promotional job for what I thought would be a nice, safe, calm place to work in a wholesome family-orientated environment to keep the peace with my husband, I had in fact walked into a place where, if my husband ever knew what went on in that company, he would have killed me on the spot. What with all the sex and drug taking that went on among the bread rolls...

Even though I had run my own extraordinarily successful team prior to my employment at the store.

I had been employed as a general shop floor assistant on the clothing section, just filling up stock, which you had to lay out to a diagram. That was a laugh – you would come in the next day to find the night team had just put stock in any old way they liked. When I confronted the lady who had filled up placing items any old place, asking her why she had filled like she had, and not used the diagram, I was asked what a diagram is!

In my case and some of the other girls on days, if you did not follow diagrams, you were given a warning before you had time to spit.

In the case of the night filler, her face obviously fitted because no action was taken against her.

You would roll into your shift after a change in diagrams the day before, which took you all day and a lot of work to sort, to find clothes just shoved any old where.

I stayed behind to talk to the other night fillers only to be told no one had showed any of the night staff how to action diagrams.

I spoke to the department manager informing her the night fillers had not been given the information or training to enable them to action a diagram, only to be shouted at and told to mind my own business. Guess what? Some of the night fillers were family members of the department manager.

This manager was held in extremely high esteem by our company, so much so that when they built a major new store just outside the city, she was chosen to run it. When she left, as was usual a stock take took place to round up the existing manager's figures.

There was a massive discrepancy on the books which could not be explained.

Six months after her departure, the department manager who had been held in such high regard at our store was sacked from the company, having been found at the new store with a car full of stolen stock. It was part of the company's rules that if a staff/store search took place for any reason your lockers/handbags/cars were part of that search.

That explained the discrepancy in our stock take figures after the manager left our store, as when the stock was found in the manager's car at the new store, the police were called in and her home searched – a massive amount of goods belonging to the company were unearthed at her home.

It was very humiliating, considering my previous job role, to be treated and spoken to, not only with disrespect, but basically as if I were an idiot and sneered at if you questioned why a thing had to be done a certain way, when you had offered a manager an option which would be more productive done another way. I soon learned managers at the company, especially in the 1990s, didn't like people offering solutions as it made them look bad. Very much the 'I am it, you're shit' way, and still to this day it continues but not as blatant now. So to keep the peace at home I had to knuckle down and get on with it.

Many a morning you would come in to find a pair of old shoes skilfully placed on the section where shop lifters had helped themselves to a new pair the night before and just walked out of the front door with them. In those days, shoplifting gangs would just walk into a store and lift a whole rack of designer jeans and walk out with them.

If you saw them come in, you were supposed to call management, but no management ever answered that call as the code used was instantly recognised and as this gang would threaten you with knives or follow you home – as happened to one girl who worked with me – and threaten not just you but your family, no chicken shit manager was ever seen to come in answer to your call.

To be fair, all shop assistants should get danger money when dealing with the public. The hours were long, and staff were expected to graft like you had never grafted before.

The rules were ridgid, uniform was strict – if you came in with the wrong colour socks on you either bought more and changed, or went home and changed, without pay for the time it took to get back from your home. If you had pierced ears your earrings could not cover the end of your ear lobes. As with all walks of life, there were exceptions to the rule. As was proved by the girlfriend of the stock control manager wearing long dangly feather earrings and getting away with it, while my stud earring with rhinestones not over the end of my ear lobes I was told to remove as being too glittery. I compared mine to the girl's feather earrings – why me and not her? – and I was told to shut up and do as I was told or face a disciplinary. That old saying, if your face fits!

Not to mention the stock control manager whose girlfriend had the long dangly feather earrings was a married woman, not only was she having this affair with the stock control manager but turned out she was bisexual and the pair of them actively approached several female members of staff with a threesome proposal, myself included. Which I found absolutely disgusting. It was bad enough I was abused daily in my home life. I never knew from one minute to the next at home if my husband would pounce, demanding sexual practices which turned my stomach just to think about never mind do. He would constantly demand anal sex, which I would constantly refuse, and he had once forcibly raped me anally, an experience that traumatised me. I learned how to avoid that thereafter, though his response was if you loved me, you would let me; my response was if you loved me, you would not even ask. So when I got that request from the stock control manager and his mistress, it literally horrified me, but because of the goings on at the store no one would listen to any complaint if you did not have a witness, and even then you didn't know if the person you had taken your complaint to was one of their threesome gang, so head down and carry on, just don't be anywhere they were on your own if at all possible.

All staff were watched like hawks by management, breaks were monitored, and at the end of shift a manager would be waiting by the clocking-out machine to ensure no one went home a minute early.

These were the days before automated tills, when every item in the store had to be priced by hand, so when a customer got to the checkouts every item had to be punched into the tills manually by the cashiers, a slow laborious process.

The store manager was a nice guy, despite his nickname (Pocket Billiards) so named by the staff for his habit of walking around the store hand in pockets playing with his genitalia as he walked. I really do not think he realized he was doing it. Not something that in this politically correct climate today he would have been allowed to get away with.

He was a well-balanced guy, who knew his staff inside out, as well as his job.

The managerial strata in the store was Pocket Billiards, then two under managers, one female Ms Hitler, so called because she really was the kind who would talk to you nicely then stab you in the back as soon as she turned around.

She had gotten where she was by sleeping with a superstore manager who was extremely well thought of; he would write all her placement letters' notes, and training briefs, enabling her to rise within the company.

It was blatantly obvious that no matter what because of her relationship with this superstore manager her career was set.

Her attitude did not affect me because of the way I lived at home, having to deflect my husband's attitude, it was something I was used to daily, so we rubbed along.

Because of my skills running a large team of people across a vast range of merchandise prior to my starting at the store, it was not long before I was noticed.

My skills caught the attention of the upper management when our store went fully automated, with barcoded stock, and scan and pack; this was in the early 1990s.

We had a couple of container classrooms on the car park where staff were taken a few at a time to learn about EANs, short for European Article Number, the codes on all stock items you see in stores today, and how to scan items into trollies, so the customer could pack as you scanned, so much faster than punching all the codes into a till.

All the tills were changed for the ones we still see instore today. And all price tickets had to be hand removed from all stock currently instore, ready for the live launch of the new way of selling.

It was while doing this training that my expertise shone through; Ms Hitler stood observing me, and the help I was giving to some of the other staff.

She approached me and asked how much training I had had – my reply "the same as the rest of the staff here today".

The next day I was summoned to the manager's office and offered a job on the Deli counter with a view to a supervisor's position in a few weeks.

Little did I realise that I was a weapon in Ms Hitler's arsenal to oust the current Deli supervisor, who Ms Hitler really disliked.

Why she had it in for the girl I do not know, but as soon as I started on the Deli, Ms Hitler made the girl's life truly terrible, picking on her in front of other staff, giving her warnings for various things which really did not warrant a warning. It was not long before the girl asked to step down from her supervisory position.

I was then made supervisor, and to be fair the counter sales soared under my management. So much so that after working at the store for a total of seven months, I had moved from a general assistant position to a supervisor then came another call to the manager's office where I was offered the position of Produce manager, which I took, even though I had to work for three months on my supervisor's wage to prove I had what it took to be a manager. Something which these days could not happen – in those days you either took what they offered, you proved you were worth your salt, or you left.

Plus, the Management money would come in very handy at home.

What I did not know was Management were expected to work all the hours extra for no overtime rendering my money less per hour than a general assistant got.

One of my Deli girls said to me: "I bet your pay packet's well heavy at the end of the week with all the overtime you do." At that time my usual hours were from four am to open the store up to a lot of days nine pm at night, this was way before the twenty-four hour stores you see today, and before Sunday openings became the norm. I told her managers were expected to work all hours with no overtime, but it did make me think – in those day though you either did it or you stepped down or left; there was no wriggle room, unless of course you were one of the 'in with the in-crowd' mob.

Once again, my department sales soared; my skills with selling and staff management increased sales vastly. I was held in high regard by Ms Hitler and Pocket Billiards.

Sadly, this was all about to change. Pocket Billiards was promoted to a much bigger store, and Ms Hitler was in a relationship with a superstore manager who was moved to another part of the country and she went with him.

It transpired that the guy she was with wrote all her references for her, so she was guaranteed an advantageous position no matter what happened.

That also applied to some individuals in various departments across the store.

A bakery youth, who had caused a major problem with cannabis in store when he was high from smoking too many spliffs, added some of his stash to some bread rolls because he thought it would be a funny thing to do while under the influence, unbeknown to his bakery manager.

A customer purchased the rolls, smelt the product, and returned it to the store manager.

A staff search took place and cannabis was found in his locker.

The lad was called into a disciplinary meeting consisting of the store manager, Mrs Obnoxious (cash office manager) and dismissed straight away. Good job for the store that the customer hadn't gone to the police with the item in one way, but in another allowed for yet another cover up, because as the lad said to me as I escorted him from store after his dismissal, "it really doesn't matter, my mother is the Head of Human Resources for the company, no matter what I'm guaranteed a job anywere within the company, no matter what I do, when I get home she will place me in another store"!

Two days after his dismissal I went into the bakery looking for an item for a customer only to find Mrs Obnoxious and a bakery youth rolling up spiffs. When I questioned Mrs Obnoxious, her reply was

"I knew they still have a stash, he is making me these for home"!

Alongside the movement of our store manager and Ms Hitler to another store came a full store restructuring. As I found out over the years, from time to time the company would do this, not so much as to keep up with changing times, but also as a tax write-off, and a way of shedding people who did not or would not conform to their hierarchy So we had a new store manager and personnel manager, and all department managers were forced to reapply for their jobs. You must remember this was some thirty years ago, before such things became the norm.

The new manager that came in was a favourite of our new area manager. We learnt that this area manager chose his team by how clean their shoes were, so you could wear the same pair of smelly knickers for a month but if your shoes were clean, it was all good.

I kid you not. The new manager's teeth were as green and hairy as I'd ever seen. His personal skills were non-existent. I can honestly say he was the most horrible man I have ever had the displeasure of having to work with in my life; he made my life pure hell for the two years he was at our store.

He was a complete and utter bastard; even the new personnel manager told him in front of all of us managers in a meeting, that he should be ashamed of the way he spoke to and treated us as she would not treat her dog the way he treated us.

I had to give her credit for that.

With him came this young flashy new personnel manager and a spare; the poor lady who was our present manager was told her services were no longer required and given a choice of leave or be sacked. Her crime? She was overweight and did not suffer fools gladly; in other words her face did not fit.

In those days, the Unions did not have as much power as they had previously had after the Thatcher years.

In the two years Mr Green Teeth was at our store he systematically constructively dismissed twenty-seven supervisors, managers, and senior team managers. He would pick on one until they could stand no more and left. Systematic constructive dismissal.

One had a profoundly serious breakdown because of him and ended up having ongoing Mental Health issues for a long time after leaving our store.

I was stood in the gallery one day doing a stock check; its main view was onto the back door. I watched as Green Teeth reduced a male manager to a heap of blubbering tears with a vile vitriolic verbal attack and a few good shoves as well. The guy's crime? He had broken his leg, and Green Teeth had forced him to come into work on crutches. These days such a thing could not happen with Health and safety rules, but in those days, it was like being under the thumb of Caligula – managers did whatever they liked with staff.

One of Green Teeth's favourite things to do was if you were on a day off, he would get a manager to ring your home consistently until you answered, tell you there was a problem with your department and demand you come in to fix this elusive problem.

It happened to me a couple of times. Once he told me the packets of cakes should be in such a straight line you should be able to roll a coin along them. This in full hearing of two senior managers who asked him if he was serious but drew the line at challenging him over his straight-line statement; they wanted to keep their jobs.

Lesson learned after that – when on a day off you would take your phone off the hook at home.

Woe betide you had a family problem on that day off as no one could get hold of you.

Pure tyranny.

On another occasion I watched from the same spot as he bollocked staff trying to unload cages from an HGV at the back door, all the while shouting the vilest threats at them as in his view they were not moving fast enough.

The corridor that the staff had to navigate from HGV to shop floor was lined with metal-covered pillars, and one of the guys was so flustered he misjudged his way and sliced the back of his hand off against the pillar.

I was a first aider, so I ran to help. The bones of his hand were showing and there was blood all over the place, including covering my blouse. An ambulance was called and the guy had to have a long operation to repair the damage.

I told him if he chose to make a complaint, I would be his witness.

It went no further.

There were some fun bits in the first few months of his stay at our store, as his lover came with him from his previous store. It turned out she was one of the new personnel managers, the other one the flashy young chit of a girl being our new personnel manager proper, we called her Ms Sparkle Pants who turned out to be the area manager's bit on the side.

Both were sent with him to our store to, as it was told, await a posting to a new store – just an excuse for him to have his totty with him, as it was unheard of for personnel managers to be moved from their original store to a small store like ours to await a posting.

This lasted about a month until the day the wife turned up at the store to confront the lover and we had a stand-up cat fight in the staff restaurant over him – why I have no idea… his green teeth and personal hygiene, or lack of, being considered.

Unless he was gifted in the bedroom department! Who knows.

To top it all off, one of my staff members had a sister who worked at his previous store, the sister had actually bought her house from Green Teeth, but upon moving into his ex-property, they found they had to replace the entire kitchen floor, as Green Teeth's dog had been kept in the kitchen and unbeknown to the purchaser at the time, the dog had been pissing all over the kitchen floor for what must have been some considerable time, the urine had seeped under the kitchen floor covering and not only rotted the floorboards but the joists as well. It was a good job they raised the floor covering when they did or the whole kitchen would have collapsed. It cost them thousands to repair.

After the cat fight the lover was moved onto another store the next day, and all staff were instructed via their department heads not to repeat any information on what had occurred in the staff restaurant to anyone in or outside of the store, on pain of dismissal. They may as well have pissed in the wind over that instruction.

In between all of this we had occurrences such as, one cashier had a tummy upset, Green Teeth would not allow her off the tills to use the ladies, but gave her a bowl to be sick in while she served customers. Serious breach of health and safety, not to mention Hygiene. And total humiliation for the cashier concerned.

Such was the absolute power of these so-called managers in those days, some thirty years ago when I first started at the store. No matter what the provocation, their rule was absolute.

One elderly regular customer was so appalled at his treatment of the staff, he told Green Teeth if he were younger, he would have offered him out as Green Teeth deserved a good thrashing for the way he was treating the lady cashiers, after observing Green Teeth's treatment of the cashier who was being sick, and other instances as a regular customer he had witnessed.

He was not wrong.

Then there was the customer who came in and asked for a couple of boxes. I gave her some, but Green Teeth called me to the office and gave me a warning because, as he put it, "a customer was stealing store boxes", the same boxes we put out for customers to freely use daily.

The man was truly despicable, and no one would stick up for you in case they were next in the firing line.

Then we had his best mate as night manager; he was London-born and the staff called this best mate Cockers, one because he was from London, a pun on Cockney; the other reason was, he could not keep his cock in his trousers, oh my God!!!!

This man was supposed to be responsible for filling the store at night.

We managers would come in the next morning to an empty store, but when you dared to question why the store had not been filled, who got the rollocking for that? Not Cockers, but us the individual department managers

Turns out Cockers would spend most nights either in the staff restaurant ordering in takeaway food, and playing games on the video console, or at his lover's house, who was one of the night time shop floors fillers.

They would come back into store just before Green Teeth's arrival the following morning, whereupon Cockers would curl up on till one for a kip after his rigorous night of sexual gymnastics –more exhausting than his actual job of night-time shelf filling.

Green teeth would feel the bonnet of Cocker's car on his way in and know full well what had been going on.

We as staff all wondered why padlocks were put on all the staff restaurant windows – god forbid if there was a fire – but that was to stop Cockers having food delivered via the windows and more importantly instead of going to the front door to let staff in upon arrival to work in the mornings when they rang the bell. Cockers was so damn lazy he was making staff climb through the restaurant windows to get into work Obviously if a worker had an accident climbing through the window the store would have been liable.

So instead of Cockers being disciplined as he should have been, he was once again left to continue doing as he pleased.

This continued for some time. We managers could not say anything – if we did, we were given short shrift or became the next one to experience harassment. So, it was heads down and continue.

Until the day the giant arrived. He was from a lengthy line of store managers; his dad and grandfather had all been store managers for our company.

He was as sound as a pound so it was not long before he saw the situation. As he said to me, he would do something about Cockers, but he had to do it in the right way.

A little while later we day managers arrived instore to find Cockers suspended while Green Teeth was on annual leave.

Giant had been summoned into the store the previous evening by a supervisor, as Cockers had sexually assaulted a female filler in the goods lift.

He was caught red handed, and the supervisor rang Giant instead of Green Teeth to deal with the situation, as by that time all the store staff were aware of the nefarious goings on, Giant came in and suspended Cockers on the spot.

Giant had to inform Green Teeth (protocol), sadly Green Teeth had not gone away but was holidaying at home.

He came into the store, summoned Cockers in and gave him the option to resign, which Cockers did. Green Teeth then rang another friend in a big London superstore, and got Cockers another position so he was free to continue his nefarious capers at that store.

Again, wheels within wheels.

That old saying: 'It is not what you know but who you know'? His lover went with him, so she must have believed whatever tale he spun regarding the move, aided by the fact he had gone from one job to another.

Giant was furious but as he said to me, at least he has gone from our store.

I felt sorry for the female staff in the store he was going to.

Cockers was not the only manager carrying on illicit affairs at our store. There was the day I went into the plant room. This plant room was a real hideaway; if you did not know what it was, it basically looked like a large cupboard door in a wall flat along the side of some stairs, a bit like the Tardis from Doctor Who once inside.

I went in this room on a weekly basis to switch off my fridges for cleaning only to be confronted by the Stock Control Manager and the Clothing Section Manager in the actual act right there in front of me! God, I do not know who was more embarrassed, them or me; both married but not to each other.

Then the fresh foods manager was caught in my provisions fridge late one night with a cashier, trousers around ankles. Brought a whole new meaning to where is the salami, I can tell you. He must have been made of stern stuff as it was really damn cold in that fridge.

But I digress.

Senior managers came and went regularly just the way the Company moved people around.

The young personnel manager Ms Sparkle Pants who had arrived at our store with Green Teeth soon moved onto bigger and better things – as she was the area manager's lover, she had a thing she wanted.

I mentioned the dress code was ridgid – in those days even personnel managers were supposed to wear a company suit. Ms Sparkle Pants wore skirts up to her bum, blouses down to her navel in a variety of day glow colours and make-up applied with a trowel.

I was filling on the shop floor; as I worked my blouse came untucked and Green Teeth saw me and I suffered a verbal tirade over it in front of numerous customers. He was literally incandescent with rage, almost foaming at the mouth while he railed at me. I couldn't get a word in as he raged so badly spit flew out of his mouth. I was given a verbal warning over it, not so much for the fact my blouse had come untucked but because I had the audacity to try and answer back to him. I confronted Ms Sparkle Pants, I asked why I had been treated so badly when she did not conform to company policy, and her reply was Hubert (area manager) says I can wear what I like, this also answered the question as to why after a social evening out for some reason or other at the store, she was allowed to roll in very late still drunk, and be treated with kid gloves, given paracetamol and told to lie down in the nurse's room to recover, while a young lady from shop floor who had also attended the same function, but who had got into work on time very drunk, was sent home with no pay and told if she did not get back to work later that afternoon and work through the night to catch up, her work would be instantly dismissed.

Her husband contacted the store saying he was taking the store management to a solicitor, and he was laughed at for trying to stick up for his wife.

Absolute power in those days, and even now it still goes on.

So, we now had to have new personnel to replace Ms Sparkle Pants and a new senior team manager to replace Cockers.

In came we will call her Ms Disciplinarian because she could make a disciplinary out of scotch mist if she did not like you.

And a manager to replace Cockers, we will call him Ferret.

From separate stores miles apart. What we did not know at the time was they had both worked at the same store near to our city 'but had been having an affair' – when found out both had been moved to different stores.

Chance happening turnabout, they both ended up working in our store where the affair resumed. They were found out by one of my staff who was on a sick day being pregnant and her husband took her out to a lunch a mile from the store, only to spot Disciplinarian and Ferret snogging in the same pub they were at. My girl informed me what had happened – as any lady who has had a baby knows, a bit of fresh air and a late light lunch is beneficial after morning sickness, so I dealt lightly with her, admonishing her to tread lightly in future.

However, Disciplinarian must have been panicking having been spotted in a compromising situation by my girl, so Disciplinarian summoned my girl to her office telling her off but could not do much else under the circumstances, having been found in a compromising situation herself.

My girl told me she had been surprised Disciplinarian had not given her a warning, but had termed the interview in such a manner as to make it clear if my girl kept quiet about what she had witnessed, Disciplinarian would leave her alone.

This was very out of the ordinary, so I did some digging with various contacts in other stores, which is how we were able to confirm their affair.

On top of that, Ferret not only had an affair with Disciplinarian but had wandering hands the same as Cocker's.

Our cash office was on the first floor. It was only staffed by one girl a few days a week. The cash office staff would have to come down to shop floor level to deliver to Securicor as the safe was on the ground floor, fed by a chute system which deposited bundles of notes straight from the cash office to the safe room. It was Company policy that a manager and the cash office girl were both supposed to sign off on Securicor uplifts. If this did not happen it automatically resulted in a disciplinary, as a lot of cash was stored in there, too much for one person to manage.

The cash office girl was in there with Ferret. Securicor had left when he proceeded to assault her, grabbing at her boobs and ripping her blouse. She managed to evade him for a few seconds, enough to fling open the door onto the shop floor, so he was in full view of the staff.

Goodbye Ferret: he could not wiggle his way out of that one; several cashiers saw exactly what was happening. The distraught cash office girl ran straight into the arms of the checkout manager, and under the circumstances the Company were left with no option but to move him on, to many witnesses.

We never did find out if he was relocated or dismissed. It went dead quiet about him, so we all assumed he had been moved up country and Ms Disciplinarian never mentioned him again.

The cash office manager lived just across the road from our store. She lived with a chap, but they were not married; she was an obnoxious woman but quite in with Ms Disciplinarian.

The cash office manager – we called her Ms Obnoxious because that is what she was – was having relationship problems with her partner. The girl who worked in the cash office whom Ferret had assaulted had an extensive list of boyfriends, but as a single girl that was her prerogative.

Ms Obnoxious split from her partner around this time, and we had a new senior team manager arrive at our store to await a posting onto a permanent store. Ms Obnoxious and cash office girl both made a play for this new man. Cash office girl seemed to be winning the race, even going out on a few dates with this new man, which Ms Obnoxious really didn't like; it culminated in Ms Obnoxious trying to get cash office girl the sack for serving Securicor in the safe room on her own, as to try and get a member of management to help you was like going to the dentist to have teeth pulled. Cash office girl wasn't stupid, she took the signing sheets from the safe room, on which Ms Obnoxious had plainly done the same thing against company policy, and signed off Securicor by herself. Ms Obnoxious could not very well get cash office girl into trouble and the sack for doing something against company policy that she was doing herself.

It all culminated one evening when the staff were attending a leaving function which both those women and I went to. Cash office girl was with the new man, and an argument broke out between them in the corridor to the venue. All three were stood together. Cash office girl stormed off, and I thought new man would go after her, but he did not. Then I realised Ms Obnoxious had her hand down his backside, holding onto his trouser belt, stopping him from following cash office girl. The next day I asked her why she had done that, and she informed me she had told new man that cash office girl was a slut and he was too good for her, that Ms Obnoxious was a far better partner for him. After that Ms Obnoxious and new man started an affair.

During this affair, on Ms Obnoxious' day off she would phone him at work and invite him to lunch at her home just across from the store. As she put it to me: "I gave him three minutes to eat his lunch then fifty-seven minutes to fuck the arse off me."

She also told me he was the Manager who some years earlier had killed a pedestrian when drink driving a company car. All the stores had heard about it, but no one knew exactly who he was. The company had told him if he kept the company's name out of the court case, they would reinstate him at the same level as he was at prior to the case. He served three years in prison, then walked straight back into his job.

Even though Ms Obnoxious knew all this, it did not stop her from allowing him to stand in our petrol station at night where security was at a maximum, drinking beer from bottles with her standing right next to him, thereby condoning what he was doing. We could not say a word as Ms Obnoxious was in so thick with senior management it did not matter what we said, it always came down on the side of Ms Obnoxious and this drunkard.

Ms Obnoxious and the drunkard did not last long together – because of his drinking he could not control his bladder, and Ms Obnoxious would wake up of a morning to find his side of the bed made after he left her home; she would just tweak her side tidy and come into work. That night she would get back into bed only to find the reason he made his side and shot off before she woke was because he had wet her bed, and she would end up rolling around in his piss.

She told me that was not so bad, it was the fact he would not own up to it that got her mad. I cannot count the number of times I would roll into work only to find this drunkard was supposed to have opened the store, which we managers did on a rota basis, only to find at say seven am in the morning the store was still shut, when it was supposed to have been opened at four am, to allow bakers in, and back door staff to take in daily deliveries.

I would roll up at seven am to find staff all over the car park, delivery lorries queued up a mile long at the back door, and him still in a drunken stupor in his bed. I would drive to his house, take forever to knock him up, obtain the store keys and go open the store.

Would he get a disciplinary? Of course not, he was not to be touched! The reason the store may have given him his job back, to keep their name out of his crime, but that became a two-edged sword to the store – he knew all the shady goings-on within the store, from who was cheating on who, the store Manager's shady backdoor deals with local small stores, and the cut he was taking on providing them with cost goods that were on promotions.

At that time, we would get cages of smashed stock in from the warehouses, which consisted of broken crates of alcohol. These would be written off for insurance purposes, then sent to stores were they would be boxed up into units of twenty per case and sold to staff cheap. The store Manager would get a female Manager to cut open boxes of an expensive beer he drank and put them into this breakages cage, so he was paying about £2, for a case of beer that should have cost £10. The boxes she trashed of the expensive beer would be charged back to the warehouse as arriving at our store broken in transit.

The female manager told me all this as I had taken a box of damages that had been made up into one of these staff cases; unbeknown to me it was the expensive beer Green Teeth had had her thrashing for himself. She had to come to me and explain why I couldn't have it, but proceeded to tell me all about the scam as I was reluctant to hand back what I'd bought without a reasonable explanation as to why it was such a problem.

On several occasions after that I witnessed her doing the same thing for Green Teeth, so he could get his freebies.

Green Teeth was also putting false claims into the store insurance company for fridge failures which never happened. If he got wind by a tip off from his connection at the insurance department that a team were coming into store to check this faulty fridge out, he would get the store maintenance man to disable the fridge, remove a vast amount of stock, which would be crated up and stored in a chiller out back. Obviously it would start to defrost as soon as the team had been in and checked the fridge or freezer failure; the stock was then supposed to be compacted as a claim had been submitted to the insurance for the stock.

No, it would then be sold off to staff at a reduced price, and the money was put into a box which then made its way to his office. We are talking of high cost goods here, whole legs of lamb, fillet steaks, you name it, the amounts were staggering – one freezer could hold thousands of pounds worth of stock, couple that with the alcohol cages, and the strong spirits that were thrashed each week, it was easily five hundred pounds a week in his back pocket from breakdowns and breakages alone.

Not to mention the promotion stock which the store would be told about weeks in advance as going on sale. He would bulk buy then contact local little shop keepers sell to them at the difference between cost and full price and pocket the difference. As far as head office knew, it was all going through the tills as promotion, as lists would be kept and actioned on actual promotion weeks when in fact it had left the store the same day as it came in weeks prior to going on promotion.

The little shop keepers were none the wiser.

Just another of his back pocket schemes.

This was also the case for another Manager caught putting goods into his car on night shift; because correct procedure had not been followed when he was suspended from the store, he also walked straight back into store in a management position some two years after his suspension, which is how long it had taken the union to get him his job back.

Again, that old saying it is not what but who you know. This Manager was put onto night shift where he proceeded to start an affair with one of the young girls in the garage because he was Asian and his family extremely strict. We all knew it would not come to anything, just a sowing his wild oats scenario while waiting for his family to procure his Asian bride from back home, but the garage girl in question really thought he was going to marry her. Boy oh boy did it cause trouble.

The Asian manager was supposed to go over to the garage at night to lock it down, but because she was on shift, he would make all the garage staff wait until he could be bothered to stroll over. This caused stress and tension among the garage girls who were married and had husbands and children waiting at home.

I tried to calm the waters by talking to the Asian chap and explaining the situation. He did not want to know, in fact it made it worse as he took a gleeful attitude towards as he termed it to me keeping his 'white slut on her toes'. By wondering if he was going to bed her again any time soon.

I went to Green Teeth with the problem, his attitude was boys will be boys and if the garage girl was stupid enough to let him shag her, she was getting what she deserved.

I could not believe it when he said that. It was causing uproar amid the other garage girls as they were all locked in until Management let them out.

This Asian manager sacked a checkout operator who was silly enough to be caught by him scanning low-cost goods while bypassing high-cost goods in a weekly shop to a family member. The cost of the shopping this cashier was scanning should have been a couple of hundred pounds but was coming out around twenty pounds. That is why one of the Company rules then became if you shopped with the company, you must not go to a family member to have your shopping processed.

Considering this Asian manager had already lost his job once before for stealing but had got his job back on a technicality, you would have thought he would have cautioned this cashier before summarily sacking her, having been in the same position himself.

It all ended when once again the Asian was caught with a boot full of stolen goods by a senior manager on his way into work one morning earlier than he should have been; he caught him red handed. Not only did they find store goods in his car but also a hoard of cannabis the size of a brick – this time he was dismissed correctly. Plus, it solved some of the mystery around where the store staff were obtaining their dope from.

It was around this time Green Teeth started really picking on me. We had all witnessed his systematic abuse of others, but being naive you think if you are doing your job correctly all will be well. No one considers that you are dealing with a sociopath.

It was not as if he was subtle about it. One day I approached him on the shop floor while he was talking to his under Manager with a customer query I just did not have the authority to action. His response was "fuck off because you fuck me off." I don't know who was more shocked, me or his under Manager by that response. The under Manager told him you can't talk to staff like that, but his response was I will say whatever the hell I like, there's the door if you don't like it.

It was a short while later we had a new garage built at our store. This was the early 1990s and a way of the company trying to corner more of the market by giving customers all they needed in one place.

I had worked in petrol stations prior to my employment with the company before my promotional team job.

I was therefore the obvious choice to run this garage.

After my promotion to Garage manager, where I had trained all the staff and associated staff in all systems concerned with running a garage, and given a co job as checkout manager as well, Green Teeth's victimisation of me kicked up several gears. I could do nothing right no matter what I did, I was not allowed a break, or lunchtime, I could not even go to the loo without him sending someone to chase me out.

One of the garage staff, a young girl, wanted a night off to go to a concert, so she asked me if I could fill her shift for her. My reply was I will try but as it is a late-night weekend, I know I am going to find it hard, so please try to fill it yourself and we will meet up again to discuss. This was a common practice – the company rules stated if your manager cannot fill a shift and you can, do so and inform your manager accordingly.

I tried all avenues to fill that shift but could not find anyone, so told the girl the only way I could let her off was if she managed to fill the shift herself.

The next day I was overseeing checkouts, terribly busy, no staff, all calls I put out for reliefs to tills were falling on deaf ears. Next thing I know I am summoned to Green Teeth's office, and upon entering saw he had a written warning already written out on his desk telling me I was not doing my job correctly and he suspended me on the spot.

I was very shocked and upset, so much so I had a bit of a breakdown and had to have a month off work. The Union came in and wiped the floor with him, turns out he had given instructions via the personnel manager for all reliefs to ignore my calls that shift, found out by the union upon interviewing said reliefs. My suspension was expunged from my record, and he was given a warning by the union.

You would have thought he would have laid off me at that point, but no, made it even worse. Upon my return to work I was immediately hauled over the coals for not allowing the young garage girl to take that shift off, she told personnel I had refused point blank to accommodate her and that she had asked me several times in the month of October about filling her shift for her.

I told personnel it would have been impossible for me to have refused her several times in October as I was absent from work for the whole of that month on sick leave after being suspended.

I also cited several people who I had either asked or had been in our presence when explaining the company system. I was then told well if it were your daughter, you would have wanted her to be allowed time off and my reply was she's not my daughter she is an employee and I observed company procedure, do I have to get the union back in over this?

No more was said about it. But by this time my nerves, my self-esteem, my confidence was non-existent.

I was also by now suffering increased abuse at home from my husband, whose favourite term of endearment to me all day every day was:

"You ugly fact fucking cunting bastard sick bitch see a psychiatrist."

And this for no reason at all – I only had to look at him sometimes and he would start. To have to live like that both at home and now at work as I was the next Manager in the firing line for Green Teeth's victimisation list.

The least little thing at work would be upscaled to a major incident by Green Teeth.

Then the garage staff dropped the safe key down the back of the safe again. I was given a warning as I was told you knew they had done that. For god's sake how was I to know as I was not there, but when the garage staff informed me what had happened, I solved the situation.

Then the night I was sorting a problem at the garage I got a call from the store. One of the cashiers had a problem with her till conveyor belt. I was the only manager on both checkouts and garage so I called the maintenance man to her till. He put a gadget on the belt to enable it to work, but this gadget gave the cashier an electric shock. I was also a first aider so I called an ambulance. Little did I know when reporting an electric shock it automatically sends the fire brigade as well, so within a few minutes we had ambulances, the fire brigade and all sorts at the store.

They took the girl to hospital and the fire brigade examined the till. The gadget the janitor had put on the till's belt was illegal, but as I am not a janitor, I had no idea. I had filled in the accident book as to what had taken place.

Green Teeth called me to his office and tried to blame me for the whole event, including applying the illegal gadget to the till. He even tried to say I had forged the accident book. Luckily I had a witness in the form of our local police officer who happened to be shopping at the time of the accident and had assisted me with the cashier concerned.

He told me to my face if it had not been for that, he was going to sack me, blaming me for the whole event.

Then there was the lady who fell in the store and broke her arm. Her husband was furious, saying the floor was wet. I called another manager and we accompanied the husband to the site of the accident but there was no sign of any wetness anywhere on the floor. I filled in the accident report and explained to the husband that I was sorry, apologising and telling him our insurance department would be in touch. Later that day I was summoned yet again to Green Teeth's office, where he yelled at me, telling me I had not done my job right as this husband had been on the phone yelling at Green Teeth over his wife's accident. I produced the accident report signed by myself and the other Manager. Green Teeth could not argue with that. A while later we saw Green Teeth pushing a super high laden trolley of goods to this husband's car. When I went back instore I asked the manager who had co-signed the accident report what had gone off. Well, Green Teeth had given the husband a trolley full of goods as a way of persuading him not to take the accident any further, but by giving him what amounted to a bribe he had admitted responsibility. We later found out the husband had sued and got an out of court settlement for injuries sustained to his wife, saying we had wiped up the wet from the floor before he had chance to point it out to managers, even though it had been put in the accident book that we had not seen any wet, by offering the bribe he had accepted responsibility.

The area manager that had appointed Green Teeth moved areas. This meant we had a new area manager come along; he came into our brand-new garage and gave me a real grilling over systems and training procedures.

My knowledge had been learned prior to my last job before starting at the store. When I had worked in petrol stations, on top of that knowledge for which I had obtained a diploma in petrol station management. During the setup of our brand-new petrol station, I had travelled to various massive stores at points over the country to increase my knowledge in a working station environment, to ensure the staff I was putting into our new station had up to the minute knowledge.

This new area manager had grilled me to find out if I knew my stuff; turns out he was extremely impressed with me. So much so he told me if I left at any point, he was worried no one would be able to run the station as well as me.

So much so, once again I was promoted; not only was I tasked with the running of the new station but also the checkouts in the main store.

That did not go down well with the checkout manager in the store. Instead of seeing it as a help to her, she took umbrage and saw me as a competitor, and once again it was that if your face fits scenario. Alongside Ms Obnoxious with whom she was best friends, they started a campaign aimed at getting me the sack.

We had security guards who they would get to do tasks they really should not have been doing, for example going into the main safe where all the cash office money was deposited to bring out cashback amounts for cashiers to deposit in their tills for customer use.

I queried this practice as obviously I was new to checkouts, but it did not ring true that these guards could do that, especially considering the Securicor sheets having to be dual signed.

I was told in no uncertain terms it was allowed, as they used these guards for a lot of things they were not supposed to be doing and had for years.

As a newbie and with no training material available for my new role, I just had to take their word for it.

I had even gone to Ms Disciplinarian, to request any training manuals on checkout procedures, only to be told none were available and to train myself.

My reply was would you say that to a brain surgeon or an aeroplane pilot?

No help with my training was given.

This went on for a couple of weeks until one day I was summoned to Green Teeth's office, and informed I was under investigation for adversely using the Guards for allowing them access to the checkouts' safe along with failing to maintain checkout schedules.

I informed Green Teeth I had done as the original checkout manager had trained me to do, but he informed me I was lying, that she had told me to do the exact opposite and never allow any Guard into the safe room on their own.

I was shocked to the core. I knew that the checkout manager did not like me, that she saw me as competition, alongside Ms Obnoxious her best mate, but had not realised how vindictive they were being.

Green Teeth suspended me on the spot, which he could not do again against company procedure.

I left the office clutching my suspension in my hand in complete shock. As I made my way to the changing rooms to collect my coat, one of the security guards stopped me.

He told me they had all been summoned to see Green Teeth and that Ms Obnoxious had told him what he had to say, that she had followed him around the store kicking his ankles as he walked all the while repeating, you will say what I am telling you to say.

He asked me what he should do. I replied just tell the truth and tell all the other guards to tell the truth as well. I had nothing to hide. Yes, I had used the guards to do jobs that I had queried with the senior checkout manager as being what I thought wrong for them to do. But as she had been adamant it was something that had always been done, and she was training me, I had no recourse but to follow her guide.

I was summoned back the next day, only to be told there would be no further action taken against me, but no apology or anything. It transpired that on the day I was sent home all the guards had been interrogated, by Green Teeth; they had all to a man told the truth about the way things were handled by the senior checkout manager and Ms Obnoxious.

Both of whom had been chastised by Green Teeth, but neither had been disciplined.

My suspension was torn up by the union, otherwise it would have stayed on my record for a year.

Green Teeth really did not like doing that; it could have caused me problems in the future if I had not got the union in to resolve that.

My fate was sealed. You would have thought having been caught out they would have laid off me, but no, it made things a million times worse.

For example, I would be left to run checkouts at the busiest times on my own instead of as it should have been with the two other experienced managers. At times with no staff, then get bollocked by Green Teeth for not meeting flow times for customers.

When I put calls out for relief cashiers to checkouts none would come. I would then be bollocked by Ms

Disciplinarian for not doing my job correctly, only to find out that she had instructed all relief cashiers not to answer my calls! When I challenged her over this her reply was Green Teeth had told her all reliefs were to be used to complete a project for him, but she knew this was part and parcel of his objective to get rid of me – without the reliefs to help on tills it was a physical impossibility to maintain customer targets.

Wheels within wheels, by doing this it was another excuse to once again haul me over the coals. All the while he was targeting one of us managers, the others knew they were safe; as one male manager told me, we knew he was targeting you, so we knew we were safe.

At that time on a Monday, we would all have to attend a manager meeting. It was while at one of these meetings Green Teeth made us aware of a fraud being perpetrated by a group of people across the country.

This group would go into a store or store petrol station and spill a product on themselves – in a petrol station that would obviously be petrol. They would then demand money from the till to have their clothes cleaned.

Green Teeth assured all the Managers at that meeting that if we followed procedure and used the insurance and accident claims books within our store, our insurance department would deal with the situation if this group of thieves targeted our store and Green Teeth would personally support each individual manager targeted by this group.

A couple of weeks later, I was called across to our petrol station. An Asian lady was saying the petrol pumps had blown back, spilling petrol onto her clothes and shoes.

I apologised to the lady all the while aware there was absolutely no petrol smell arising from her person, no visible signs of damp patches on her clothes or shoes, all this in full view and hearing of the garage staff. She demanded thirty pounds from the garage till to get her apparel cleaned and purchase new shoes. This was in the early 1990s so thirty pounds was quite a bit of money.

Following procedure, I explained we would have to fill in both an accident report and an insurance claim. We could not just give cash from the till, so would she mind accompanying to the main store to fill these reports in. She agreed.

As we walked across the short drive to the store, she told me she had heard you could put shoes in the washing machine to clean them. I replied please do not do that, just let our insurance deal with it for you, all the while knowing this was the fraud Green Teeth had warned us about.

We actioned the forms again in full view and hearing of the customer service staff as that was where these books were kept in store.

I reported the incident to my immediate superior and left it at that.

A couple of days later I was summoned to the naughty chair again by Green Teeth. Upon my arrival in his office I was informed that the Asian lady had put a complaint in about me, that I had been rude, I had frog marched her across to the main store to fill in forms.

Once again, a suspension form was already written out on his desk, but this time I fought my corner. I informed him nothing had taken place like that, that staff both in the garage and the store had witnessed the event and my handling of it, had he bothered to investigate prior to summoning me to his office.

He was furious and told me to leave. I was suspended. He also informed me: "This time I have you, there is no job for you anywhere within this company."

I left the office and went straight to the staff who had observed the incident, got them to write out there and then what had happened, rang the union and informed them of the current situation, and started towards my car only to be stopped by the girl who used to be Deli supervisor prior to me.

She told me she knew what was going on, not because word spreads like wildfire within a store, but because her boyfriend knew a store manager in a local small town outside our city; it just happened her boyfriend had gone to school with this manager; her boyfriend had told her that the manager, his girlfriend and Green Teeth were best mates. Green Teeth had asked this girlfriend to perpetrate the event in our garage where the girlfriend had supposedly spilled petrol on herself and to demand my presence to resolve the situation, I still don't know to this day if Green Teeth told them of his ultimate aim to try and use this event as a ploy to get rid of me, or if he told them it was a training exercise, as obviously all stores or so we thought would have been aware of the country-wide scam taking place with the gang trying to obtain money for spillages scam.

The boyfriend had come home and told the ex-Deli supervisor all about it. He did not know who I was but was shocked at the duplicity of it all, bearing in mind how she had previously been treated by our same manager. Green Teeth would not have known who he was, just another faceless person to Green Teeth. But the boyfriend knew who he was all right.

I asked her if she was willing to give me a statement regarding this incident. Her reply was: "No problem. I am leaving this store next week, I have secured a job with another employer so no one here can harm me anymore. I just wanted to make sure Green Teeth cannot continue doing to you what he has done to so many others here at this store."

I have never felt so much gratitude to another person in my life as I did to her at that moment.

The union contacted Green Teeth and arranged a meeting between himself, our personnel and me. Upon entering the meeting, Green Teeth was so full of himself, he was positively gleeful, until all the staff statements were placed in front of him. He still tried to blag it out with the union, who had advised me prior to the meeting that may happen. The union asked me to leave the room then informed Green Teeth if he didn't allow me to step down from my management role into a full time garage supervisor's role, of which there was a position available within the very garage I had set up, but keep me on management money, they and I would take him to tribunal.

He knew when he was defeated. As a consequence, I started my new position that very same day. He had to explain to his area manager the reasons why this was happening, and why he had to keep paying me management salary. That really did not go down well with the area manager, but it would have meant dragging the store through a court case, which would not have gone down very well at all with the company.

The knock-on effect for Green Teeth was he started to be the one being persecuted by the area manager – now he knew how it felt, the absolute swine.

Now I was stationed in the petrol station full time I had a clear view of the whole carpark and the store from the station. Green Teeth would always park his car in the same spot; the girls in the station and myself had a running joke that if we won the Lottery, we would buy the parking spot he used and ban him from parking there.

One day as we watched from the window of the station, a customer parked in the spot Green Teeth used. Upon Green Teeth's arrival at the store you could see he was fuming about the car in his usual spot. A few minutes after his arrival, the deputy manager came across to the station and said to me, "Can you go and move your car?" I never connected at first so asked him why I should move my car.

He said Green Teeth was raising hell in store, "he has gone round every Department, yelling at staff, accusing them of parking in his spot, but now he knows it's your car he is incandescent with rage. He knows you have done it to spite him because of the Union getting the better of him in letting you step down".

I said to the manager, if Green Teeth comes and asks me himself, I will move my car, at which point the manager said, "Please do not ask me to go tell him that, I really cannot stand any more of him today, he is making everyone's life in the store miserable, and he has only been here a few minutes."

I took pity on the manager and said that is not my car in Green Teeth's usual spot. I do not think he believed me, but as it happened, as I said that the owner of the car came along and got back into the car. The manager was very shamefaced, but apologised to me and said, "You know what he is like, he is so petty, like a child having a tantrum."

Another good thing that came of me being stationed in the new garage that I had put all the systems in and trained all the staff to use, was that my expertise had become known to the wider senior managers.

I was then asked to start training other stores' staff in the running of petrol stations, not only in our hometown but from far and wide. I trained staff from Scotland, Wales, Amersham, Newcastle, Rugby, Stratford-on-Avon to name just a few places. All of this added to my status to such an extent that stores having new petrol stations were waiting in line to send staff to me. This went on for some time until we had a few petrol stations up and running who then started training other stores' staff in their associated areas. Green Teeth really did not like it that I was being held in high regard within the company, but after the last run in with him he dared not cause me any more stress.

It was around Christmas time when this last run in with Green Teeth had happened. We had trouble finding a venue to take our store for its annual Christmas party, as the store had previously been banned from several venues for bad behaviour at these events.

We found a social club just up the road from our store for the Christmas event that year.

I attended without my husband as part of my department's group. Most managers were there including Green Teeth with his wife, and Ms Obnoxious, who had been given charge of the petrol station as a figurehead – we never saw her at the garage unless there was a problem with cash deposits. Most staff that worked at the store attended. The actual party was coasting along nicely, and I left the event room to pop to the loo, only to bump into Ms Obnoxious French kissing a married department manager just outside the ladies' loos. Things were getting quite heated between them, but as I came back out of the loo they had disappeared. I stopped to speak to a member of staff and her hubby; as I did all hell broke loose in the men's loo, which was just up a bit from the ladies' loos. A senior manager came boiling out from the men's loo, clutching both Ms Obnoxious and the guy she had been kissing by the arms, both of whom had their clothing in disarray. Turns out Ms Obnoxious had been caught red handed having sex with the guy in the men's loo!

By this time, I should not have been shocked at anything, but I was. The senior manager called another manager passing by and told him to fetch Green Teeth. Upon his arrival he told them both off and ordered them home. Turned upon his heel and stalked back into the event room. The guy went but Ms Obnoxious went back into the ladies. I continued to speak to the couple I had been talking to when it all kicked off. Ms Obnoxious walked past us, smiling as if nothing had occurred, but as she turned the corner she let off the fire extinguisher on the landing and broke the fire alarm. This automatically summoned the fire brigade. In the following melee it turned out as she had made her way to the outside of the building, she had let off several other fire extinguishers en route.

What a commotion! Fire engines, staff and event personnel not knowing it was a false alarm.

As Green Teeth got his wife to their car outside the venue, he caught one of the shop floor lads urinating on his car, all the while boasting to the mates with him that he was doing it because that was his opinion of Green Teeth.

The next day at work, Green Teeth made the youth wash his car and gave him a written warning which stayed on his record for a year.

As for Ms Obnoxious, absolutely nothing was said or done to her after all the melee she had caused the previous night; the married manager she had been with, however, was given a caution by Green Teeth. Nevertheless, it was the beginning of the end for Ms Obnoxious.

Little had we known, but Ms Obnoxious was bisexual. Not long after the Christmas party melee she came to the garage to talk to me about garage changes. While talking she told me about her and young chit personnel's times in her bed in-between her affair with the drunkard, both of whom had been gone a while by this point. Once again, I was shocked. I really did not know whether to take what she was telling me with a pinch of salt... until she put both her hands on my breasts trying to massage them while telling me she had always fancied getting me into her bed! Shock after shock! I quickly disengaged from her, telling her I was not made that way, this time I would let it pass but do not do it again.

I do not think any of the girls in the garage believed me about that occurrence.

That is, until every member of staff and management witnessed her pull up one day in her car to the store with whom we can only assume was her current lover, a female, and she proceeded to French kiss this woman in full view of the store, bearing in mind I am talking over thirty years ago when all this type of thing was still very much frowned upon in society.

A manager sent a guard out to her car; he knocked on the window and instructed her to stop and move along. Her reply was to stick two fingers up at him and the store and start to undress the woman. At this point Green Teeth went out and sacked her on the spot.

The next day our area manager came instore. From our vantage point in the office next to Green Teeth's office, we could hear every word being said. We all thought it was to do with his sacking of Ms Obnoxious; turns out it was in a way but because of Ms Obnoxious' high jinks at the Christmas party.

The social club where we had had our by now notorious Christmas Party had informed head office of the Christmas party melee and the subsequent bill for damages to the venue. There had been an investigation which had not only turned up what had gone on at that event but the four years' events prior to that where local venues had put in complaints about aberrant behaviour including managers pushing bar staff about, removing drip trays from behind bars and drinking the contents then throwing up all over the bars. I had witnessed that event myself; it was appalling. Also, staff going through people's pockets in cloakrooms, stealing the contents of said pockets and being caught... the list goes on.

And the fact that our store had been banned from every venue in our city for the foreseeable future.

But also, the goings on in the car park the day before, the area manager was incandescent with rage, and this time it was Green Teeth who was sacked on the spot.

Result!

Could not have happened to a nicer man, the absolute swine. Pity it had not happened sooner and saved all those other managers and supervisors from his tyranny.

In the two years he had been at our store, he had systematically gotten rid of twenty-seven poor souls.

So once again we had a new manager; however, I was not around that store at that point to see what went on.

As the day after all this kicked off, I was summoned to Ms Disciplinarian's office where she proceeded to apologise to me about all that had gone on with Green Teeth, saying she had been in total fear of the man. I could understand that.

Also, that she had acted the way she had to preserve her job and offering to make me back up to a manager, stating I was too good to be left at a supervisor's level. I agreed but told her I wanted to be at a store more local to my home, so within a week I was posted to a store just around the corner from my house.

For anyone who has ever been in an abusive relationship of any kind, they would understand that this move of store to me meant not only a fresh start at what I thought would be a smaller store, therefore with less carryings-on among staff concerning extra marital affairs, drug taking, and downright dishonesty not only at shop floor level but even more so at managerial level, giving me what I perceived to be some peace of mind at work at least; but would once again most importantly appease my violent husband as now I was literally a stone's throw from our home, so he could drop into the store at any time to assure himself I was actually where I said I was, which once again I thought would make him realise, I was not, as he continued to tell me, having affairs.

These types of men have such an overwhelming control of the person they are abusing, it really is a vicious cycle; it takes a real catalyst for the victim to wake up and escape their abuser's hold.

There was one time I had, in my innocence, started to tell him about some of the goings on at the store, only to have him fly into a rage, accusing me of being involved with all of these goings on.

To say I was shocked and astounded at his behaviour when I was talking to him about these events was nothing compared to the attack that then happened a few seconds later, as I had continued to talk to him, saying "hang on, I'm telling you about these events because I'm shocked by them and asking your advice on how to handle, them not that I'm involved in them". He flew at me, shouting, "you ugly fat fucking cunting bastard sick bitch, you're telling me you're shagging this person", while putting both his hands around my throat, proceeding to choke me. I clawed at his hands futilely; all I could think was I'm going to die. I managed to scream and my then young daughter came running into the room, shouting "Dad, Dad, what are you doing to Mum?". It gave me that second's release as his grip loosened to stagger away, dragging my daughter to me. This must have given him a second's clarity as he spun and left the room. I honestly know if it had not been for my daughter that day, I would not be here to tell the tale. I prayed with all my heart she would never remember that event.

I was wrong again.

From that day on I never told him of anymore of the goings on at my previous store. I was not stupid enough to add fuel to a raging inferno that was his delusional psychosis of anything I said or did.

And now at a new store I felt much calmer, perceiving this store to be less of a den of iniquity.

Oh my God, how wrong was I? My sense of calm did not take long to abate.

So, I not only had a horrific home life to contend with, but now another tumultuous work environment also. Through the years at my final store I cannot stress how many times I was reduced to a pile of sobbing tears by various trainee managers.

Young inexperienced people who were callous in their handling of staff to try and further their own careers.

So, as it was a much smaller store but as a manager over all fresh foods, in some ways it was a promotion for me and to my husband a lot fewer males in the store for him to suspect of having affairs with me; in fact, this store compared to my last store only at that point had one male employee in 67 staff members and the store manager, compared to some 10 to 15 men employed in my previous store which had a total of around 350 staff members.

Companies' stores even to this day are mainly staffed by female employees.

Ms Disciplinarian oversaw personnel for this store, my now new store, and had told the store manager I was a good manager, that I would do an excellent job for him. This guy had been at this store for some ten years.

A well-established manager with the company; however, he was old school from the days of pile it high sell it cheap. It was now 1997 and the company was expanding fast and with it its image and the way it worked also had to change, so this manager's days were numbered.

Along with this established manager, a good portion of the store staff were long term employees, some having worked at this store from leaving school some transferring into this store from an old store that had been closed down in our city centre, the terms in years these staff had ranged from 20 to 40 years with the company, very unusual in our company but when you think about where the store was situated in the community it explained a lot. After my fraught years at the larger store I was hoping for some calm and peace. It did not take me long to realise that was not going to happen.

On my first day I called a staff meeting to apprise my staff of the way I liked things done. I was met with stony silence. Seeing as the store manager was long term, you would have thought things would be running smoothly; the opposite was in fact the case, things were very slipshod.

After the initial meeting I worked alongside my staff as they worked, being a much smaller store built in the late 1960s within a busy local community right on a busy local shopping centre, it was quite confined for both access for deliveries and unloading at the back door, which meant cages had to be taken straight from delivery to shop floor and worked there, then any stock not able to fit the shop floor fixtures would be taken via a really out dated lift to the second floor to a cool prep room with an old fridge for fragile stock to be stored.

in those days the store did not open until 9am and closed at 5pm Monday to Saturday – this was before Sunday opening was allowed, as delivery times to this store were also restricted being in a built up area, unlike the big stores you see these days built right on the outskirts of towns and cities, which are not compromised on time restrictions; this meant staff could not come into store before first deliveries were allowed to come in at 7.30 am and none allowed after 7.30 pm at night.

So, you only had 90 minutes to get your product on the shelves before the first customer came in. Nine times out of ten for whatever reason your delivery would be late so haste and speed really mattered, then you also had to follow the cold chain no product left out of chill for more than 20 minutes or it would become waste.

The staff worked well; however, I was shocked at the state of cleanliness. I don't think the fixtures had been cleaned in years. I asked one of the girls when was the last time this meat fridge had been cleaned as I discovered congealed blood and other debris in not just that fridge but in every fridge I worked on. Her reply: I remember cleaning it three Christmases ago. She carried on walking towards the back area of the shop, I then realised they had all disappeared, with cages of stock left scattered any old place; it was now 9.30 am and the shop had been open to the public for some 30 minutes so most if not all the stock and cages should have been off the shop floor.

I went looking only to find every member of my staff in the staff restaurant, munching their breakfast.

I went into the staff restaurant and told them as soon as they had all finished, I would like to see them in the training room. Staff were allowed 15 minutes per break; I looked at my watch and told them that would be in 5 minutes' time.

I left and went to the training room. As they arrived, I asked them why they had all gone on a break together, leaving fragile stock on the shop floor, which for one was a trip and risk hazard, and two because it broke the cold chain rules.

The reply was we have always done it that way, which explained the vast amount of stock the store was losing every week to damages.

I informed my staff that from now on they would work to the correct way of handling cold chain goods and to company rules, that breaks would be staggered, and they were to inform me when they had finished working a cage before a break was taken, and any cages or stock not worked by that time was to be moved up to the cold room while on their break, not left on this shop floor to conserve the cold chain and prevent accident.

I also informed them that the following day I would be implementing a cleaning system and cold chain checks which should have been taking place daily already.

One of the girls informed me the reason no cold checks took place was they did not know how to turn fridges off, or which cut off switch was for what fridge. So, I made a trip into the attic evaluating the equipment and labelling switches to correspond with labels on fridges on the shop floor.

You would not believe the filth I found in those fridges. Within two weeks the fresh foods waste bill had dropped by 85%.

As the company was now using sales-based ordering, whatever went through the tills automatically reordered itself – there should have been minimal waste.

This also applied to ambient grocery, or as Joe Public calls it, long-life products, tins of beans, tea, coffee, etc.

Therefore the warehouse should have been empty.

It was in fact rammed to the rafters with cages of stock, a lot of which was out of date. This explained why the established store manager was on a very slippery slope with the big bosses at Head Office.

Within four months of my arrival at this store, the established manager had been moved to a store miles away in a very rough area on the other side of the West Midlands, causing him to add four hours' journey time to his day. And a store so bad that it employed two full time security guards as every day there would be an incident of some sort needing police intervention.

The manager of that store was transferred to our store, which meant he was only 30 minutes from his home.

This new manager was young, funny and pleasant; he did, however, do a job on the side as an accountant which earned him twice the wages he earned at the company – which the company really did not like; they did not like anyone doing well outside of the store.

This young guy was with us about a year before he was pushed out of his job by the company telling him he could not do justice to both jobs. When in fact he had turned the store around, increased sales and was well liked by the staff.

My department's sales, through my cutting of waste and adding extra lines, had increased by 90% – a massive jump for such a small store.

The young manager was so pleased with me he had sent me to various meetings and conferences in his place, stating I was more than capable, and just prior to his leaving had spoken to me about becoming assistant manager as not only had I turned fresh foods around but at every Senior Management conference he had sent me to in his place, the feedback on my expertise had been exceptionally good. I had impressed the area manager who not only visited our store regularly and knew my work, but also attended the conferences where my good knowledge and expertise shone out.

Alas, alongside our manager's departure went our area manager to the new overseas Asian chain our company had just bought. It went hand in hand with a massive restructure of the way the company did things in the UK; also as our store now became a training store where future store managers were placed to make their mark on the way things were done before being moved on to bigger and better stores, some remained a few months, some a couple of years dependent on how our store traded, this being held as the yardstick for their promotion levels.

The first such trainee manager was like Green Teeth reincarnated (GTR for short as we termed him), he would give you a task then once completed move the goal posts, so you had to start all over again.

He was married but quite a heartbreaker. A new section manager was bought into store to co-run checkouts alongside an established manager who had been with the company in her position for years; the new section manager termed by GTR as a flyer was brand new to both the store and the job.

It was not long before we all realised Flyer was in fact GTR's bit of totty on the side. Flyer would leave the store, telling the girl on telephone desk, "if my boyfriend calls while I'm out tell him I'm in a meeting". Right behind her GTR would leave the store, telling telephone desk, "if my wife calls tell her I'm in a meeting". Off they would go in the same car, returning about two hours later. He would look a bit rumpled, but the clincher was the straw sticking out of her hair and his jacket at the back of his neckline – we all said considering the money he earned he could at least stump up for a hotel room and what would they do in the winter!

On top of that, on one occasion I had to follow them upstairs to the office with a situation update while they had been absent from the store. Never giving it a thought, I walked in on them in his office as he hastily took her panties out of his jacket pocket and was handing them back to her as I walked in on them both giggling like school kids.

She could do no wrong. We were not allowed to contradict anything she did even against company policy. If there was an embargo on ordering supplies for any department, which used to happen from time to time when these trainee managers were trying to impress senior managers, you couldn't even order till rolls or carrier bags – as I pointed out you can't run a store with no till rolls but she was allowed to order a three hundred pound trolley which never got used. We were all supposed to do a late night each week, not her, and the only late night she ever did I was also on shift I was running the tills, she was overseeing the general floor and back door area. I got into work the next morning on a middle shift only to be called into the office where I was told I was to be given a warning for leaving the roller back door open where goods came into store. To say I was gobsmacked was an understatement.

I told GTR go right ahead just let me get my Union rep in first. He went crazy at that but as it was his mistress that had left the store wide open, he could not do anything to me about it.

She suffered no consequences at all. When challenged over her thwarting of various rules and lack of late-night shifts, her expenditure on three hundred pond trolleys, we got told to mind our own business or look for another job. It got so bad the established checkout manger gave GTR an ultimatum, which resulted in her having to step down from her job role. GTR even tried to put her back on starters' pay instead of trained cashiers' pay.

The man was an utter swine. It became blatantly obvious it had been his plan all along to put his Flyer in the established manager's place.

Then the stock control manager had similar issues with him. She also was made to step down after we were forced to do a twelve-hour day on a company training session which took place at our store. The stock control manager's child was taken seriously poorly and her husband contacted the store to inform her of the situation. GTR had left instructions we were not to be disturbed for any reason, so her hubby came to the store to get her. GTR told her if she left the training session he would sack her. She told him but my child is poorly, and he told her it was not as important as the training. She walked out upon her return the next day after a blistering row with GTR; she also stepped down. Family is more important than work.

This left us all in a position where we knew not to rock the boat, or we would be next, such was the culture of bullying in the company of management being able to do and say anything to staff.

You toe the line, or you go. It was still a time when, according to the Company, we women only worked for pin money.

Maggie Thatcher had by this time been in power for some years – to the common person on the streets, with all the loss of various industries our jobs meant your family did not starve.

In that respect I was lucky: my abusive husband was a hospital porter on exceptionally low wages, so I was used to making ends meet and my wages certainly did not go on pin money items but kept my children fed – yet another reason not to rock the boat: I needed my job.

GTR was at our store for a few more months which meant all staff dare not do or say anything to cross him or his Flyer.

Then came a change of personnel managers to a male personnel manager. He also took a shine to Flyer, and within a short space of time she was moved to this new personnel manager's permanent store... Where she crashed spectacularly – much larger store, no one to cover for her as the male personnel manager had too much to occupy him, what with covering that large store and our small store.

Within a month she had given notice and left to work in the insurance industry.

At that time, our store layout was such I could walk along the back of checkouts through the exit door and straight into the entrance door – they were side by side.

Just inside the entrance was a kiosk where tobacco products were sold; it also doubled as our reception desk. This was only ever manned by one person.

One night I went to check on a product for a customer which was adjacent to both the kiosk and the entrance door. As I entered the door, the young girl in the kiosk at first glance, a split second look, seemed to be backed up against the kiosk wall with her hands in the air. I realised that a man was, as I thought, molesting her across the width of the counter. My gut reaction as a mother was to pull this chap back away from her. As I did so I realised he actually had leaned in and opened her till while threatening her, to grab a handful of bank notes which, as I struggled with him, he dropped. We wrestled and he ripped my blouse open, all the while trying to grab the notes which had become strewn across the floor.

I grabbed the tannoy and screamed for help, then chased him out across the street where he ran down the alley across the road behind the shops on the other side of the road. Then it hit me, adrenalin stopped pumping and sanity returned. I thought hang on, if he has a weapon, I am stuffed, I am all on my own here as no help had come from the store.

I went back to the store still not realising what a state I was in, blouse ripped, red faced, out of breath, totally dishevelled.

When I got to the store, the girl in the kiosk was slumped in the corner in shock.

All of this had taken seconds. GTR had still not answered the frantic tannoy call I had put out. As I was helping the girl from the kiosk at the same time as calling for help from checkouts, the kiosk phone rang. GTR was on it, incandescent with rage, giving me a bollocking for shouting down the tannoy while he was on the phone to our actual over manager from the large out of town store that oversaw GTR's tenure of our small store.

I informed GTR what had happened and that I was not impressed he had not answered our alarm call. He told me he did not care about the fact both myself and the kiosk girl had been assaulted and money stolen, only that he had been interrupted in his phone call to his boss. The police were called, which infuriated him even more as now his boss would have to be informed of what had happened. The police were not impressed by him at all and waited for his boss to arrive from his store. By this time shock had set in with me as well as the kiosk girl, my shock compounded by GTR's attitude and derision. I was sent home by the overall boss where my husband proceeded to give me a good slapping for coming home with a ripped blouse, never mind my assault and shock. The outcome of that was I ended up having to have a month off work with shock, anxiety and depression.

The assault, the robbery, the bollocking and the slapping from my husband was all too much. The overall boss sent me flowers at home, which was nice, but he had no idea of what his trainee manager was genuinely like, and no further investigation took place as to what had happened that day. As per usual for our company, it was all swept under the carpet – if the store was taking money that was all that mattered

Upon my return-to-work, GTR went out of his way to make me fully aware he did not like the fact he had been shown to be lacking in front of his boss; he gave me such a workload to complete, all the time being constantly on my back. If I went for a tea break, he would come to the staff room and in front of whoever was there bollock me over any little imagined slight; the same with lunch. This went on for about two weeks, then I had my first heart attack.

Again, I was off work around a month before I went back.

I really was not well enough to go back, but I was terrified of losing my job and terrified of being at home with my abusive husband. While I was at home, I had been getting late night phone calls from some woman asking me if this number belonged to the Christian Affiliation. I said no, wrong number. She then proceeded to give me my home address. I was stunned. The only way she would know that was if she knew exactly who and where she was calling as our number was ex-directory. I said who is this – she then put the phone down on me. When my husband came home the next day from his night shift I told him about the phone call. He flew into a rage, for the second time trying to choke me; this time both my children were there and my son grappled with his dad, causing him to release me, but charging across the room to my daughter who was trying to phone the police. He didn't touch my daughter, but ripped the phone from the wall cutting my daughter off. As he did that the neighbour came pounding on the door having heard the screams. That put paid to his attack as he was a yellow-bellied piece of scum – he did not want his public demeanour to be shown up for the swine he was in private.

So, the devil or the deep blue sea.

That day upon my return to work I was told to man a checkout as cashiers were off sick. To be honest, I was thankful, as I really did not feel well at all. A lot of staff were coming up to me saying you don't look well you should have stayed at home, but no one at the store knew what my home life was like and I couldn't explain. I had about an hour to go before my shift ended when one of GTR's blue eyed girls came to me and said, "GTR said you don't look well, you're to go home." At first I was shocked that he had realised I still wasn't well, but then realised if I conked out at work he would have some explaining to do yet again to his over manager, that's all he was worried about; and considering what I had actually been off sick with, a heart attack, he could have sent me home sooner. When I got home my husband was just going to work so I did not have him to worry about, thank goodness. During the night I took a turn for the worse and had to ring for an ambulance, ending up back in our local hospital. This time I was off work another month.

Again, on my return to work I was told in no uncertain terms by GTR that when he sent me home that day, he had fully expected me to return to work the next day, rather than take another month off. He then issued me with a written warning for my sick absence.

A couple of days later I was called to the office by GTR who informed me I must go to a company training session around a new ordering system. I was shocked as ordering was nothing to do with me.

I asked why me and he said the stock ordering person was going away for a period of time and I would have to take on this role or step down. I told him I know nothing about computers, you really need to find someone else, but he was adamant it was to be me. Did I want to stay employed or not? He left me no choice. That night I went home and tried to find some sort of course at the local night school to help me with computers, I found what I thought would help me and enrolled, paying for it myself

Turned out it was totally the wrong thing.

I went back to GTR and informed him I needed help. He was furious and would not help me. But I found a member of staff through the stock ordering system in another store who told me if I went to him, he would give me as much info as he could but asked me why it was being left so late when I explained what had gone on. He was disgusted; this chap told me as much as he could to help. I went back to the store only to be met by a furious GTR; once again his behaviour had been passed along by the stock guy who had tried to help me.

He had been given a good telling off, but by now my nerves were shot, my confidence had been totally undermined, coupled with the abuse at work and home.

I decided it was time to step down. GTR could not have been more gleeful; he had at last achieved his aim: all the managers in the store at the time of his arrival had been successfully demoted or stepped down. To add insult to my injury, he then proceeded to tell me I would have to work every late night on checkouts. I told him to sod off or I would get the union onto him. He was not happy about it, but considering what had gone on with hindsight he thought if I got the union in, he would have been in deep trouble. I was so traumatised I just gave up and was glad to be given a job just sat on a checkout.

Shortly after this, GTR was also moved on to a bigger store as thanks to his reduction on staff wages by making three managers step down, he had made our store look, on paper, more profitable.

He was not there long thanks to him doing a similar exercise, having an affair this time with their store personnel manager, but this time the department managers of that store went over his head to Head Office about the affair, as it was causing major problems within the store.

As no one could get problems solved because of the affair between GTR and Personnel, they were too involved to do the jobs they were being paid to do, one of them knew GTR's wife and spilled the beans to her as well. Both GTR and Personnel were fired and GTR's wife left him

We then had a succession of short term mangers. The first chap that turned up was a really good manager who was awaiting a posting to his own store, but he had been put into our store while the next manager was taking a two-week holiday before taking up his role at our store, something this temporary manager was not impressed with. Like he said, if someone offered me a managerial role I would prove I was interested by giving up my planned holiday and taking the job I had been offered.

He went on to say "but then the only reason this new manager has been offered this store is he has been on television portraying the company as a family orientated company".

That night I went home and found the programme – it was all about this new manager teaching children of the company's workers cricket, thereby portraying both the company and him as a good all-round wholesome environment to work at for future employees and to shop at for the public; fantastic publicity to generate more income for the company.

As the temporary manager said, the company could not then put this new manager back to his original position, they had to be seen to promote him; you couldn't have someone chosen to do a national television programme about the company and its so-called family ideals just left in their original role, so our store being a small training store was ideal for supposedly him being given what appeared to be a promotion – to anyone following up on this guy it would appear he had been promoted for his role in the programme, and if he was not skilled why would the company have recommended him to the television company.

Again, the company had caught themselves in a trap much like the one with the drunkard at my original store being reinstated after his release from prison after his drunk driving had killed someone while driving on company business in a company vehicle.

As I have previously said, trainee managers once in situ would do anything to prove they had increased turnover. Once that was done, the company would then give them a permanent store that could take anything from three months to a year.

This new permanent manager to be once at our store, we will call him Mr Cricket, took just over two years to be moved on.

He was not in any way a good manager from his people skills to his turnover-generating skills; in fact, when he left the store was turnover-wise taking the same as when he arrived. While he was at our store, both my son and daughter were given part-time jobs, my daughter being the older of my two children was working as a cashier, taking a year out before going on to university.

As a rule, youngsters going to university would ask the company to alter working hours to fit around any university hours, enabling them to work for a bit of pocket money while studying for a further career.

In my daughter's case they would not oblige her with a change of hours once she started at university. I had seen this happen to others before her for several reasons, but mainly that old saying: if your face fits you're in, if it does not, you are out.

I tried to help my daughter but the company has such means at its disposal to wriggle out of any situation where it would be seen to be discriminating against any one person. The upshot was my daughter ended up having to give notice so she could attend her university course. At the time it was a situation she could have done without as it caused her major stress wondering how she could provide for herself and attend university at the same time, but with hindsight it benefited her as she got a great job around her university course with a company that could not have been more helpful.

This enabled her to then look for work in the field she had chosen, Computer forensics, with job offers from MI6 along with other companies.

Touché: you never know what you have until it's gone.

My son was at this time just leaving school – unlike his sister he wanted to go straight to college to take a Graphic designers' course. He is quite the artist but like his sister wanted a few hours on a Saturday to earn a bit of pocket money.

Mr Cricket was quite happy to employ my son as a Saturday lad working on fresh foods, in particular fresh fruit and veg – this being the heaviest area to work benefited from a lad with a bit of muscle.

My son, unlike his vocal, gregarious sister, had always been a quiet, deep-thinking child – I cannot count the number of times I had to go to see my daughter's headmaster at school for whatever trouble she had gotten into that week.

Whereas my son never gave me a bit of trouble.

With hindsight, in those days children were classed as either quiet and deep, or Borstal material. Of my two, my daughter was Borstal material, my son the deep one.

When little he would lie on the floor drawing and talking to those drawings. No one at school ever picked up that he may have had a problem, being as our home life was so tense it took all my emotional skills just to keep the peace when their dad was not at work.

These days with mental health being so publicised someone like my son would be picked up at school and the parents told they may need to investigate their child.

I truly wish when I had had the courage to leave their dad when they were little I had stayed gone, but in those days schools would get the so-called professionals involved; it was the days when no matter how fractured the family was, children were seen to be better off with their parents.

These professionals some forty years ago intervened when I left their abusive dad; the long shot was my then husband promised to change to be a better man, to attend anger management courses.

My husband and I got back together; six months later I was trapped. I endured another eighteen years of hell, sadly, even though I thought I was and had protected my children from my ex-husband's terror, the emotional and mental health impact is and was something you could not see happening, but took a massive toll on not only my children but myself also.

Mr Cricket took a shine to my son, offering him a full-time job. To be fair, my son was a good worker, held in esteem both by staff and section managers alike.

There was an older woman working in stock control; this woman lived with her partner with whom she had a young child and they were engaged to be married. Not long after my son started at our store, this woman changed departments to work on the shop floor.

At that time, I was organising some first aid training courses and this woman asked to be sent on one of these courses. While talking to our back door man about the course and who was going on the session, he told me this woman was rare and to be wary of her as she could cause trouble. I had not heard the expression before so he elaborated – it meant she would go after anything in trousers. I knew upon my arrival at the store there had been trouble with the late-night checkout manager having an affair with a staff member, resulting in his dismissal from the company, but I had not realised it was Ms Rare that had caused the problem. Caught on camera in the cash office having sexual relations with the night manager, she had also sent letters to this man's wife telling her all about their affair, resulting in the wife descending on the store in a fury, confronting not just her husband but the store manager, who at that time had been the old school type manager, who would not in any way condone such goings on and had summarily dismissed the late manager but could only give Ms Rare a warning as it could not be proved who had actually written the letters. And although caught on camera in the cash office, Ms Rare's face was obscured, and being in uniform the staff all looked the same, so it could not be proved it was her conclusively, so she managed to keep her job but got a warning.

As I had no reason to prove otherwise, Ms Rare never having given me any problems, I told the back door man whatever had happened it was in the past, but I would be wary, so I sent Ms Rare on the course…

Only to have her return a week later to tell me she had, while on the course, had a one-night stand with the instructor. I was shocked, back door man proven right

I asked her what about your partner, and her reply: it happens, it's done now.

It was about a week later I was walking past the open back door to our store, open because Securicor was at the safe removing cash, when I saw Ms Rare come out of the Securicor van door. This was a shock as those vans are just as stated secure, and when asked what have you been doing, she replied "snogging", bloody hell!

A while later we had an ex-night manager from the days when our store ran a night shift return to us on days for a short while, awaiting a posting. Turns out Ms Rare and this man had also been having an affair while he had been on nights at our store; it seemed her nickname was well earned.

Ms Rare came to me one day telling me she had lost her engagement ring and her partner was really upset about it – had anyone found it? I said no but would look out for it and ask about to see if anyone had found it. I jokingly said to her, you can always get a new one, but she replied, "no I can't, my partner won't buy me another one after my confession". I asked her what she meant, and because she was upset and off guard, she told me she and her partner should have gotten married the previous month, but she had wanted to start her married life with a clean sheet so had confessed to him all the affairs she had had, at which point her partner had cancelled the wedding, telling her now he knew all about her (pre) extra-marital affairs he could not trust her and did not feel he could go forward with the wedding, but for the sake of their child would stay with her, so this ring was the only one she would get. As it happened, when I went to our staff restaurant for my break later that day I had a good look around and found her ring under one of the tables in between the wall and the leg of the table. She didn't even thank me. I think it was because she had told me too much and regretted it.

Mr Cricket was interviewing for a security guard for our store and he employed an Asian chap who seemed quite nice, down to earth and pleasant.

He did his job, although to be fair I never ever saw him apprehend a shoplifter in all the time he was there, and he also was not much of a deterrent as the local wide boys seemed to be on best terms with him.

However, this security guard soon became best friends with Mr Cricket, going out to meals with him, staying at his home at weekends for parties etc. One of the Asian cashiers had two daughters working at our store; they had a friend, also Asian, whom they introduced to the guard and within a short space of time their friend and the security guard had started a relationship, which resulted in an engagement.

All the staff thought it a real love story.

While the guard's main job was security, he was also trying to start his own business and, as most Asians do, he had a finger in quite a few little side lines. His cousin who used to visit him instore was a member of our local police force, a Detective, and the security guard was desperate to make more of himself and had applied to join the police force.

At this point my son began slacking off from his college course, playing hooky. I tried to talk to him about it but couldn't get to the bottom of what was going on. He then told me he wanted to take a year out and work full time at the store, as you do. I said, "Well ok, if you do go back to college after a year."

My son and Mr Cricket seemed to be getting along well together. Mr Cricket would be sending my son out of store on various errands for him, which I never questioned – it seemed as if my son was being coached for greater things... Until the day the security guard's supervisor came instore. He asked me, "Have you seen my security guard?" I said no so he went looking. My son had just returned from yet another Mr Cricket errand, and he also had disappeared. The supervisor came back to me a few minutes later. Grabbing me by the arm, he took me to one side. He had found all three men – Mr Cricket, the security guard and my son – in the disused boiler house which the majority of staff did not even know existed, where there was a long wooden work bench used by the maintenance man for various jobs. Mr Cricket was using the bench to cut up lines of cocaine with a staff discount card which the security guard was inhaling through a rolled up bank note; my son was just outside the room looking on.

I immediately found my son and asked him what the hell was going on. He told me Mr Cricket had been sending my son out to source this and other drugs for him. It turned out that one of my son's ex-school mates had turned into a drug dealer, my son and Mr Cricket had been talking one day about stuff in general and the subject came up, Mr Cricket telling my son he dabbled, asking my son if he could go to this ex-school mate and source Mr Cricket some drugs. So all the errands my son had been on for Mr Cricket were in fact drug runs! I was bloody furious, telling my son he was a bloody idiot – if caught, he would be the one in trouble, not Mr Cricket. My son said he was caught in a honey trap – he knew he had been a fool but didn't know how to extricate himself.

I told him no more errands. I then went to Mr Cricket and told him in no uncertain terms "my son will not be running any more errands for you". Trouble was, because I did not see the actual transaction and did not want my son to get caught, my son and I were now between the devil and the deep blue sea – no concrete proof. And the security guard's supervisor was in the same predicament. It was and still is to this day because of the way these stores work very difficult to prove wrongdoing, and if you could prove wrongdoing, Management being in league with security and other higher management, unless you called the police and reported these events, without major proof all you are doing is putting yourself in the firing line for victimisation and constructive dismissal.

It appeared after that Mr Cricket left my son alone to just do his job, while the security guard and Mr Cricket got chummier and chummier, not only spending time together at work chatting, but the guard would spend weekends at Mr Cricket's house attending various events, some with his fiancée who loved to regale us all with the facts upon her return to work.

The fiancée was, it seemed, not a bad sort, but it soon became apparent there was friction between her, and her two best mates, the other two cashiers employed by us. It all came to a head a couple of days after the security guard went missing from his shifts one week, along with both the two cashiers and the fiancée.

I was summoned to Mr Cricket's office to be told I needed to train up three new starters on checkouts as the fiancée had left due to finding the security guard in bed with both the cashiers, one of whom had resigned, the other one was taking some time off. The one who was taking time off had replaced the fiancée; in Asian culture this was a massive insult to the fiancée whose male relatives were actively looking for the security guard and the absent cashier, even coming into our store demanding to know where the guard was. It was quite scary.

Mr Cricket had a real problem sorting that one out. After about a month the guard and his now new bride returned to work, now married to each other. Her mother who still worked for us was really not happy with that situation; her sister, the other cashier also involved in the ménage à trois, had been sent away from our city to relatives for her own safety. She never came back but got married off while she was away.

The guard and his now wife were brazen about the whole thing; I could not believe their brass neck – not only unashamed but openly telling other staff their (love story) talk about try before you buy.

For a while, this occurrence had taken my mind off my son and what he was up to. He worked well but had been going out of store for his lunch and tea breaks, which seemed unusual, but I never thought much of it. The security guard by this time and his new wife seemed as if they had sorted out all their family issues so at work everything seemed to be settling down, while at home my husband was getting more and more abusive – if I was not getting verbal and emotional abuse, I would be getting deathly silences that could last for weeks. These were more unnerving in a way as it was usually the calm before storm, I was always walking on eggshells.

Then came the day at work that we had the armed robbery. The then back door man, Steve, had opened up for Securicor, only to be confronted by a masked gun-wielding gang. They marched him to the stairs which led to our cash office waylaying the chap coming down from the cash office with a case full of cash. These cases usually held somewhere in the region of ten grand a trip, from cash office safe to Securicor van by way of these stairs.

My son was working on the shop floor when a customer rushed in through the front door yelling that we were being robbed at the back door. My son, the customer and a female member of staff all gave chase to the robber, who, thank the lord when he saw three people chasing him, dropped the gun he was carrying and the case of cash he had snatched from the security guard. Blue dye billowed from the case as he ran away.

Steve the back door man was in shoc,k as they all were, as with my cashier robbery previously it is all adrenalin until after the event when you take stock and realise how lucky you have been.

Obviously, the police were called and they did all the usual stuff and left.

It was not long after this event I caught my son and Ms Rare in a clinch in the warehouse. My son then proceeded to tell me that he and Ms Rare had been seeing each other outside of work for some eighteen months – she was the reason he had given up College, sneaking around to meet her in various places, that they were in love.

One shock after another, if not at work, then at home as lives were woven in and around the store.

As you may well imagine, it was an horrendous situation – not only was my son at that time only seventeen and a half, but this woman was some ten years older than him and in a relationship with a child; also there was the history of her numerous affairs.

My husband when he found out was raging, proceeding to tell our son he was dead to him. What sort of father says a thing like that to his child? So any hope I had of reasoning with our son went out of the window at that point, by my husband's actions he had pushed our son right into this woman's arms. Ms Rare had spun our son a tale of abuse at home from her partner including sexual abuse, and my son being the gentle soul he is was ripe for the picking, wanting to be able to protect what he saw as a vulnerable woman he loved being hurt. My asshole of a husband, instead of being calm and talking to our boy at that point, although he didn't know it, had ended any hope he ever had of a father-son relationship.

I could do nothing to alter the course this relationship would now take. What really upset me and infuriated me was everyone in our store had known about this situation for over a year and not one soul was kind enough to tell me about it; perhaps if someone had, things may have turned out differently.

Now because my son was fully aware of just what his dad was like, plus all the pressure at work with Ms Rare telling him all sorts of lies, he began to take drugs.

Cannabis at first, then harder drugs as things got worse in his life. We were at home one night when he asked me to take him to town. Ms Rare had phoned him to say her partner had thrown her out, having found out about my son and her. Again, what do you do in a situation like that? So I took him to town to meet her, all the while praying for the best outcome, which was the night my son left home for good emotionally while still staying at home for spaces of time while fliting between our house and Ms Rare's temporary home. My son was telling me Ms Rare was upset and he could not leave her on her own.

I could not stop him. They got a place from someone my son knew that night. They both turned up to work the next day, but my son would not discuss the situation with me at all, telling me that all the affairs she had were just lies told at work by people who disliked her.

Nothing like a fool in love, they cannot be reasoned with.

Ms Rare's 'mother-in-law' descended on the store that day where a full-blown argument arose, resulting in Ms Rare being sent home with the 'mother-in-law' to try and sort out the situation. None of us wanted my son and Ms rare to be together, but she had a young child to sort out. The child had been sent to her grandmother's while her dad tried to sort out his relationship problem.

Ms Rare was determined she was staying with my son and was not a bit concerned about her child. The atmosphere both at work and at home was intense and stressed.

About three or four days after all this kicked off, I was Duty Manager when the police arrived at our store asking for Ms Rare. I showed them into the office and went to find her.

We all stood in our small office while the police informed Ms Rare that her partner had killed himself at his place of work by electrocuting himself – he had wrapped a live wire around his wrist in his shop on the Friday night, being found when the shop staff had gone into work the next morning.

Ms Rare's face never changed expression when the news was delivered. The police said she had to go with them to identify the body, and she said, "I will just get my coat and bag from the cloakroom." I followed her out of the office door, but instead of going to the cloakroom she went straight upstairs into the warehouse where my son was working, not realising I was right behind her. She walked up to my son and said, "The police are here, he has killed himself, you can move in tonight."

I was appalled at the callous cow. The expression on my son's face is one I will never forget – shock, horror, utter devastation; she did not know I was right behind her as she told my son the information that destroyed his life.

With that she turned and walked back down to get her belongings and went off with the police. I asked my son "are you all right?" but he just could not answer me. I had to go back to the office to see Ms Rare and the police off the shop premises. To this day I do not know who was more shocked, me or my son. By the time I got back upstairs he had gone; his shift still had a few minutes to run but under the circumstances I was not about to tell him off.

We never saw him again for three days. Ms Rare said she had not seen him either when I went to her home, having found her address from the store files. I still to this day do not know where he had gone to, I was frantic in case he did something stupid – you just do not know what people will do in those circumstances. His father was no use at all, he was more concerned with himself as usual and how everything was my fault, how his son was dead to him, no mention of 'I hope my son is all right and safe', no thought, care or concern for anyone but himself. Telling me as usual I was an ugly fat fucking cunting sick bitch, see a psychiatrist.

The turmoil I was in, it is a wonder I did not go insane.

Obviously, Ms Rare now had to take time off from the store to sort out funeral and childcare arrangements. My son would keep disappearing for periods of time, coming home briefly to eat and change clothes, but continuing to get to work.

He would not engage in any talk about Ms Rare and that situation. One Saturday morning I was up preparing to go to work for my shift at nine in the morning. I usually rose around seven to make sure my son was up as his shift started at seven-thirty.

I let him out of our front door, locking it behind him. Within a couple of minutes there was a knock at the door and my immediate thought was he has forgotten something. I opened the door to be confronted by six great big police officers who informed me they had a search warrant for my home and an arrest warrant for my son. I really do not know who was more shocked, them or me, when I said, "Yyou have just missed him, he has just gone to work."

They backed my up my hallway, some diving upstairs where my husband and daughter were asleep, some started pulling my front room apart, all within seconds.

The Asian Detective in charge told two of the uniformed coppers to go to my store and arrest my son. I was shivering with shock. I asked the detective what my son was supposed to have done – his reply to me was armed robbery.

My poor son was hauled out of the store we both worked at and brought back home. Police went into his room where he had all sorts of posters on his wall, one of Al Pacino in Scarface, to which he had glued a tiny plastic container no bigger than a fingernail with talcum powder inside to represent cocaine, the subject of the film Scarface – that was taken as evidence. My son was an avid Star Wars collector; he had numerous figures from the films in his collection, all in orderly named and tagged zip locked bags for each Star Wars film.

One police officer picked up the unused zip bags saying to the detective, "Shall I take these as evidence?" The look I gave them must have spoken volumes as they were suggesting by their actions that these bags were being used to sell drugs instead of the innocent purpose they were used for, protecting Star Wars figures from dust and damage.

The detective looked at me and told this stupid female copper to leave them where they were.

So apart from a bit of talcum powder and some empty plastic bags, they found nothing.

They then informed me my son was being taken for interrogation.

At this time in our area there had been a rash of armed robberies – the building society next to our store had been hit twice, causing it to permanently close. The post office and the big newsagent in the area also had been hit, along with our store.

My son was gone for over twenty hours, finally arriving back home after midnight in a very distressed state.

He said the only reason he had been let go was there had been a murder that night in our local area so all police resources had been diverted to that crime. They had let everyone they had arrested in connection with armed robberies go, all on bail. I asked my son who else they had arrested and he said he didn't know but had been told by the police that four others had been taken into custody, all sent to separate police stations in the city.

Our whole family at this point were both mentally and physically exhausted. We all turned in for the night. The next morning my husband continued to rant and rave about the situation, instead of doing what any normal father would do, at least talk to his son and offer support. My piece of shit husband not only berated me, telling me this as usual was my fault, but also his own son who was so mentally upset at being accused of an armed robbery plus the ongoing situation with Ms Rare, was a cunt and dead to my husband.

I rounded on him at that point, telling this piss poor excuse for a man that his son was innocent and suffering with both situations, how dare he say the things he was saying, he should be ashamed of himself – all to no avail.

At this point my son just walked out of the door; he could take no more.

About an hour later his sister came home. She had been staying at a mate's house overnight.

She was visibly upset, telling me that a chap both she and my son had gone to school with, the brother of her best mate, had been in their local pub the night before when someone had gone into the pub with a gun after a local drug dealer who had double crossed him over a drugs deal.

Her best mate's brother had been in the wrong place at the wrong time; he had been caught in the fire as this drug dealer and his customer started shooting at each other and he had been killed instantly. This was the murder that caused the police to release all the men they had arrested for the armed robberies.

My son also knew my daughter's best mate's brother – they had all gone to school together, and while not in the same class, they had all hung around together, being in the same year and living within a few streets of each other. So, I now had two terribly upset young people to deal with and an insane asshole of a husband who, rather than trying to help and console his children, was too busy feeling sorry for himself while verbally and emotionally continuing to abuse both his children and me.

His tirades reaching a crescendo, at which point I called the police myself – enough was enough. The police arrived just as my husband punched our son in the face, who had returned home a while after his sister, while screaming at him, saying, "it is all your fault, you're dead to me".

The police officer grabbed my husband and marched him backwards, saying, "You are no kind of father. If I see you raise a hand to your lad again, I will arrest you."

It was absolute turmoil. The police officer should have arrested my husband, my son should have pressed charges, so many should have could haves. Instead, our son just left again, leaving me broken and himself desperately broken; it was all too much for a nineteen-year-old to manage.

When he turned up the next day, my son would not give me any explanation as to where he had been. Looking back at the turmoil he was in, he was easy prey for the next move Ms Rare made.

Our son had gone to Ms Rare, who at this point was still off work after her partner's suicide, the funeral being that week. Ms Rare had repeated her offer of my son moving into her home after the funeral was done later that week. Nothing I said to him about her made any difference – a fool in love is the worst kind of fool.

My son also asked me, "Mum, what should I do about work?" My reply: "You go in as normal, you have done nothing wrong." At the same time, I really did not know what my reception would be when I got to work.

On the Monday morning my son left for work at his normal time. He was very apprehensive. I was due in on a later shift on a Monday. Within a couple of hours my son had arrived back home – he had gotten to work, being greeted as if nothing had happened, the store manager had let him fill his section, saying nothing about the police taking him from our store. My son had then put away all the back stock and tidied away all cages etc before going to the canteen for his morning cup of tea. At that point the manager asked him, "Have you done all you're supposed to do?" My son said yes, the manager then asked him to accompany him to the office where he proceeded to inform my son , now you have filled up and worked this morning's stock I'm suspending you from work because you were arrested last Saturday, no what happened , no union representative no are you ok nothing

Talk about being found guilty before being proven innocent, or hung, drawn and quartered.

Once again, my son was totally devastated.

I went to work where I was the subject of snide whispers, sneering looks and people gossiping behind my back, which would abruptly stop with telling silences when I walked into a room.

It was awful and that was just work. At home what had been an abusive relationship now tripled in intensity as my poor woebegone husband blamed me for everything in his life that he perceived as wrong, not a thought or care for anyone else in the family who was suffering, just poor him.

All the while continuing to try and force me into vile sexual practices while exhorting me with "if you loved me you would", or "I'm doing this to show you what problems your son has caused for you", throwing me to the floor as I fought him off then leaving me lying there, unable to rise due to the intensity of the force he used, like a soiled dish cloth. Then telling me as he walked away, "You do not respect me!"

At work I had called the Union in over our son's suspension. An investigation started which resulted in the Union informing the store that what they had done was out of line.

Our son should not have been summarily suspended; no one had bothered to ask my son what had happened, just carte blanche judged and suspended.

However, because of the way the Union worked, and the store did not want to be seen as having made a massive judgement error, his suspension stayed in place for a week before store management rescinded it. This gave my son time to move into Ms Rare's house.

So now I was in a position where gossip was rife around the armed robbery, then the situation of my son and Ms Rare living together – this was the stuff Hollywood films are made of.

If the store gossips knew what my home life was like on top of these two situations, my life would have ended.

The lady who ran our store cash office told me I looked really ill. To be honest, I do not know how I continued to put one foot in front of the other daily.

Amid all this emotional turmoil, the ex-fiancée of the Asian security guard who had caused such trouble at the store with his ménage à trios came in to see me; she informed me that it was this security guard who had given my son's name to his cousin, the local detective who used to visit him in our store as a way of trying to lever himself into the police force to which he had applied. That pinged my memory; I knew I had seen that detective somewhere before, but couldn't remember where.

To say it was one shock after another was an understatement. I asked her if she was sure and she said, "Yes, I am sure, the reason I am telling you is you supported me when I found out about 'Asian' and his ménage à trois. I was grateful to you for that support. I had a lucky escape with him. I did not realise it at the time, but it was."

Ex-fiancée proceeded to tell me "'Asian' and his wife are now running a big shop in Wolverhampton, employing several staff, but his wife, my ex-friend, is very unhappy as Asian is still preying on his female employees for sexual favours." The mother of the ex-friend still worked at our store but was very closed-mouthed about her daughters since they had left our store after the ménage à trios had come into the open; we knew one daughter had been sent away and married off, and of course Asian and his wife had left our store and moved away, but until Ex-fiancée visited me this day, no one knew where Asian and his wife had gone or what they were doing.

I had employed a solicitor for my son after his arrest, so I passed this information onto him given me by Ex-fiancée. He made some enquires, but the solicitor told me because it was just information about who had given the police my son's name as a suspect in the robbery, it would have no impact on the actual case. The solicitor went on to say it was a shame a person of Asian type had to resort to trying to get someone like my son into trouble as a way of gaining access to the police force, but for whatever reason the police force had turned Asian down repeatedly, so maybe being a Grass had hindered him rather than helped him, that's why he had to move towns and ended up effectively working in a shop.

When the police had arrested my son, they had taken his phone off him.

They had gone through all his calls and texts but the only thing they found was a call to one of the other men that they had arrested at the same time as my son. The solicitor asked my son if he knew this man and my son said, "Yes I went to school with him. I ring him from time to time and sometimes he rings me" - only one short phone call in a year of calls.

This was all the police had to connect my son to one other suspect.

The police investigation went on for some eighteen months which included several visits to courts where my son would be told his bail was being extended, until one day our solicitor came out of the court before my son had even gone in, saying The Crown Prosecution Service had summoned my son's solicitor in to tell him the Police had no evidence whatsoever against my son and his case was being dismissed. The other man my son had phoned, whom the police had also arrested in connection with that robbery, was also in the clear and had also been told his case was being dismissed, no evidence against him either. In fact, while all this had been going on, the spate of armed robberies had continued in our area, so obviously the police had pulled the wrong men.

At the end of this horrid situation, my son had now moved in full-time with Ms Rare, but it was a very volatile situation – as that old saying you do not know someone until you live with them.

My son soon realised Ms Rare was not only a serial man eater, having affairs with his best mate and others, resulting in screaming rows, after which I would get a phone call asking me to go pick him and his belongings up as he was leaving her... Only to arrive at her home to see my son hanging out of the bedroom window, Ms Rare having locked all the doors to stop him leaving and was sitting in front of the front door preventing him from leaving. I lifted the letter box to peep through and call her name, asking her to move. Immediately behind the letter box I was confronted with the top of Ms Rare's head and hair, it was surreal. Ms Rare never moved a muscle or acknowledged my position outside her front door. My son eventually had to scale down the side of the bay window to escape.

This situation continued for some time, then one day my son approached me at work informing me Ms Rare was pregnant with his child. I was not surprised. Ms Rare ever since my arrival at the store had professed to have been pregnant several times, not only with her previous partner but also with her one-night stand partners, then eventually professing to have either been mistaken or had a miscarriage, never supplying doctors' evidence to any of these miscarriages, saying it had been too early in the pregnancy to have seen a doctor. In my son's case, however, it was a true pregnancy.

Things both at home and work got worse and worse. Our family was the subject of the vilest gossip over my son and Ms Rare, while at home my husband was taking great glee in being even more abusive than normal, blaming me for our son's relationship with Ms Rare, I was not allowed to eat, sleep or drink without him either screaming at me over the situation or using me as a punch bag over it.

My home situation continued to disintegrate as my son had now effectively left home and my daughter had moved to Yorkshire, having met an older man with whom she was now living, eventually becoming engaged to and buying a house with, so at least at that point it seemed one of my children was settled and happy.

I thought that now the children had left home my husband would calm down and appreciate the wife and home he had. Over the years of working with the store, I had saved shares through a store scheme, ploughing all the money from them into our house, new bathroom, kitchen, koi carp pond, landscaped gardens. It was really well looked after and kept scrupulously clean by myself, my husband never lifting a finger to do anything. As he told me, women and dogs have no souls, which is why Allah made women to do menial work and bear male children.

All through Ms Rare's pregnancy with the ups and downs of our son's coming and going after each fallout and my husband telling me to choose between him and my son and our expected grandchild, my life continued to be an emotional rollercoaster.

Abuse and physical violence at home, snide comments at work.

Some months later, just before the birth of my grandchild, in our local paper there was a story about the armed robberies with photographs of the gang who had perpetrated them.

I took the paper into the store, asking various staff and management if they knew the people in the photos. Most of them did actually think it was my son. Obviously I had folded the names over so they were not visible, and as soon as one person made a comment, I would turn the paper over to show the names, blatantly proving our son had nothing to do with the Gang or the robberies. Not one single person apologised to my son or me for all the 18 months of agony and trauma we had been put through.

Even my bastard husband, his own father, did not apologise to his son; this so-called father who had told my son on his arrest he was dead to his piece of shit father.

To this day my son suffers from PTSD and in fact this trauma, coupled with his situation with Ms Rare, my son actually ended up being sectioned in 2016 and to this day is under the local Mental Health Team.

He suffers acute anxiety, paranoia and depression; he has not been able to work in over twenty years, a life destroyed by an uncaring store and company initially. And a woman who with hindsight I should have had arrested for paedophilia as my son was only 16 years old when he started at that store and she got her claws into him. Ms Rare used and abused a gentle caring boy for her own ends, subsequently cheating on him with his best mate after the birth of my grandchild, then dumping him when the next sweet young thing came along.

Our grandchild was only five months old when Ms Rare dumped her on me part-time to bring up, which eventually became longer and longer periods until eventually after social services became involved, The Family Court awarded me full custody and at the age of fifty-three, I then became a full-time mother to a five-year-old child again.

My husband all through this continued to abuse me both mentally, physically, and sexually.

In the two years leading up to my custody award, I had started to lock myself in what was our daughter's bedroom at night, with a big wooden wedge under the door in case the lock broke.

When our grandchild was around, he was usually not too bad; it was only after she went home, he started his abuse. I therefore thought my husband would calm down, being given a chance to parent a child who was not his own directly. As I have said before, people in abusive relationships become conditioned to accept that they are at fault, that everything is happening to them because they are unworthy; you hope that this time things will change for the better.

How wrong was I. On the first night we bought our grandchild home from Court, he started to berate her verbally over some stupid childish action young kids do.

I straight away removed her from his presence, telling him she only five years old – "you are supposed to be the adult".

That was the catalyst.

I had my eyes opened wide the next day. After taking the child to school I went to our local bank to speak to the manager and explain the situation.

The female Bank Manager gave me a five thousand pond loan, allowing me to rent a house. My best friend, who had known of my home situation all along, handily had three big strapping sons, all ex-services.

Within a month I had a property rented and a plan for leaving in place.

One August Saturday morning, these Ex-servicemen heroes pulled up outside our house. For the first time in about a month, my husband spoke to me normally, saying "what the fuck is that van doing outside my house?" from his usual position on the sofa where he would sit and cuss and disparage anyone passing by.

My reply: "it's for my half of the furniture, I am leaving you and I am taking my half of the furniture".

It was the first time I actually saw him speechless. The Heroes came in, not even acknowledging my husband, they started removing the items I needed to move with. I had sent my grandchild to her half-sister's grandmother for the day, so she was out of the way.

My husband never said a word to these heroes, he would not, he was only capable of abuse to those that could not defend themselves.

The heroes went off with some items in the van to the house I had rented. In-between my husband asked me, "Why did you not tell me you were leaving?" My reply was: "I have been trying to talk to you for years, especially in the last few weeks since our grandchild arrived full time. You would not speak to me or even acknowledge my presence unless it was to either verbally, emotionally, physically or sexually abuse me. All I have had from you over the years is violence of some type on a daily basis, most terrifyingly most of the violence has been in stunning silence as if you are a robot.

"The only time anyone realised just what you are like is when your only friend and I arranged your work leaving do and you forgot just where you were and who you were in the company of, when upon my arrival at that do with your cake I had made, you charged me, calling me a fucking bitch for not telling you about the surprise. Those men were shocked and appalled to such an extent that they chastised you publicly telling you 'God, man, that is your wife to whom you are speaking!'."

At that point, my husband rang his only friend asking him to come to the house as there were men all over the house removing his furniture.

When his friend arrived, he asked me what was going on so I told him. His reply to me: "I knew this would happen one day, I did tell your husband he is out of order."

My husband then rang the police who, when they arrived, I informed them I was leaving my husband and taking half the furniture. My husband told the police the heroes had pinned him to the floor and threatened him, my gasp of shock and the expression of amazement coupled with my expression of 'you bloody liar' must have told the police all they wanted to know. They informed my husband I had every right to leave and to take half of everything. The police then left.

Not long after the police left, the Heroes returned, taking the rest of my belongings. I left that house, a house I had put all my Company share monies I had saved, my wages, my heart and soul into, without a backward look. The sense of freedom was amazing.

It did not last long.

Within a brief time, my husband had employed a solicitor, telling this solicitor I was a danger to my children and my grandchild, that I had been locked up in a Lunatic Asylum for a period of time.

That his daughter was an alcoholic prostitute, and his son was a practising heroin addict.

You must understand that while I was being accused of these things, I was also being asked to prove beyond a shadow of a doubt by way of my medical records and various other avenues to the courts and legal people that these allegations were in fact false.

My soon to be ex-husband although asked at one point along the way to provide evidence to not only support his claims against me and his children, and on the other hand refute the fact that years before we had got to this stage, he had in fact been told he was to attend anger management and that psychiatrists very much wanted to interview him, stating to me people like your husband are kept locked up in Broadmoor. Never gave to any legal person one shred of evidence to support his wild accusations.

It proves the male dominance of the era and these situations when my then husband never presented one piece of evidence to the courts, yet I had been put through the wringer.

Unless you have been in this situation, there is no way anyone could imagine the turmoil, stress, and anxiety a woman suffers, to such an extent many a night I could not sleep, resorting to driving around the city in my car in the early morning hours just to try and gain some sort of peace for my stressed-out mind and body.

Our daughter's relationship had at this point ended; she had been with this chap for five years. She had moved back to our City and I had offered her a place with me, but because I had a three-bedroom rental where myself, my son and his daughter, my granddaughter now lived, I could only offer her a sofa bed. I also had nowhere to store her furniture and other belongings she had.

My daughter at this time was thirty years old when she returned to our city. She told me, "It's ok, Mum, I will go back to Dad's," our ex marital property, "and just keep my head down."

That did not fill me with confidence but as she was an adult, I could not do anything other than agree.

Our daughter stayed with her father for around two months. In that time she obtained employment as a manager with a massive well known insurance company that had a huge office in our city; she was doing really well.

At her father's house, our daughter was given a ten pm curfew by her father – if she was not in by ten at night, at age thirty, all hell broke loose.

Now she was experiencing what I had gone through for years. Until the weekend – she told her father she would be staying over at her long-time school friends for the weekend; these girls had been at school together and kept up the friendship for years. Her school friend was having a BBQ family event, and my daughter was invited to her friend's BBQ; it was a bank holiday weekend.

On the morning after the friend's event, my daughter arrived home to her father's house to find the door locked and bolted from the inside, so she rang the bell. Her father opened the door, dragging her inside by her arm while taking her door key out of her hand. My daughter was obviously shocked and stunned as to what was happening. Her father was raging, telling her she was a prostitute for staying out all weekend.

He then proceeded to kick her repeatedly in the back and threw her out into the street.

She rang me very distressed, explaining what had gone on. I went and picked her straight up, taking her to my home. I then rang this worthless piece of shit excuse of a father, but before I could get a word out, he started to rant and rave down the phone.

I cut in, informing him I was reporting him to the police for assault, which I did. The police subsequently arrested him and questioned him.

When he returned to his house, I rang him again. This time he was more cautious although still ranting, as now he was becoming aware his time of tyranny was ending. He told me he was going to throw all our daughter's stuff in the garden and burn it. I informed him I still owned half of that house, and while I did our daughter's stuff would remain in my half; if he did not want to be rearrested, he was to leave her stuff in my half of our ex-marital property alone.

I also told him I would be around the next day to pick up her clothes. When I arrived the next day with our daughter, he had his only friend there as a witness, which I found ridiculous as neither myself nor our daughter wanted anything to do with him, we just wanted her clothes. We went upstairs to her bedroom. As we proceeded up the stairs you could plainly see he had fitted padlocks to all the upstairs doors, even the bathroom, to prevent us from entering any of them.

How ludicrous was that, as if we would have gone into any of them – we had no need to.

But it just showed the way his mind worked.

Our daughter stayed with me for some time until she got her own place. At which point once again I had to beard the lion in his den, this time taking a van to move our daughter's belongings from our ex-marital property. Once again we were met with padlocked doors and a pile of boxes in the hallway as well as her furniture and his only friend in residence.

We didn't ask, we just took the stuff and left. When we got to her new home and started to unpack it was to the realisation that her father had smashed every single thing he could that was contained within her boxes, the absolute bastard. I wanted to get the police involved but my daughter said no, she just wanted to forget her dad. From that day to this, some thirteen years later, my daughter has never spoken to her father, even after giving birth to my youngest granddaughter. I have broached the subject and her reply was "why would I put my child through meeting or seeing him, he's vile". I can't say as I blame her to be fair.

So now we were at the point where my husband had no one to abuse, everyone was away from him in their own homes, but my ex was determined we were all still to suffer. He continued with the court case he had employed his solicitor for. This court case took some three years to resolve, not only had he told his solicitor I was a lunatic and his daughter an alcoholic prostitute, his son a heroin addict, but was spreading rumours all around the neighbourhood consisting of details of the case.

These things take time to investigate and myself, my son, my granddaughter and my son's ex-partner all had to attend the offices of CAFCASS, where we were all interviewed.

I will never forget the social worker who interviewed us; he introduced himself to me, informing me he had met my husband earlier that morning. He then stated that my husband was throwing accusations out all over the place, my reply: I am not at all surprised.

His reply to me: "Well I can tell you now your husband has shot himself in the foot. I just gave him a box of tissues and left him to it."

I replied to the social worker, "Should you be telling me this? I am supposed to be the bad guy in all this."

During the investigations it was deemed that my ex could have visitation rights to our granddaughter a couple of days a week, which the child was not happy about, but under the circumstances I had to try to explain to her I could not do much about it.

At that time, we were in a situation where my granddaughter had a half sister who lived with her paternal grandparent on a court residence order, her mother, my son's ex-partner who was now actually married for the first time to a chap with whom she had a baby son, so it fell to me to try and arrange for these three siblings to meet up once a week. Taking into consideration work commitments for four households to what was sometimes a herculean effort, my husband would nevertheless demand his time when he wanted it, no matter what anyone else had to contend with. I had to try and explain to courts and social workers that my husband would have to work around all these other households' commitments, him being the only one who did not work, it seemed to me to be reasonable and that I would try to accommodate him as best I could.

It was a Saturday afternoon. The grandchild had been at his house since early morning; her siblings were coming to visit as planned that afternoon, everyone was aware of the arrangement. Her mum turned up, still no sign of the granddaughter. I rang my husband, who told me, "I am keeping her, you are not having her back." I said, "Her mum's here as arranged." As we spoke her sister arrived with her grandparent. I asked her mum to accompany me to my husband's house to pick up the child. When we arrived my grandchild was visible through the full glass door at the front of the house, visibly distressed, while my husband ranted through the glass front door telling me "you're not having her back". As I knocked on the door again, he flung the door open, dragging me inside. I just had time to say to her mum call the police before he slammed the door shut. My grandchild flung herself at me, hysterical; she was five years old.

When the police arrived, a female officer came into the house. She was very unprofessional, telling us we should not be fighting in front of my grandchild, totally missing the fact that my husband was standing in front of the door, preventing me from leaving.

At that point a male officer came into the house, looked at me and my grandchild, and from the state of the child and my expression he could clearly see the problem. He spoke to my husband who was ranting and agitated. As he spoke he was backing my husband up the hallway away from the front door, so I took full advantage of that, picked up my grandchild and flew through the door. As I did my husband tried to grab me, dragging me off my feet, wrenching my arm really hard. I did not look back but heard the male officer tell my husband to "let go or I will arrest you for assault". To this day I thank the lord for that male officer's common sense and clear judgement of the situation.

When the case eventually went to court the social workers' report totally exonerated not only me but our daughter who was doing so well at her job her company wanted her to move to their head offices in Devon to head up a new department.

My son who had admitted he had dabbled with drugs, was now under a rehab programme and was clean. The Judge castigated my husband in front of the whole court over my son, telling him as a father "it's your duty to help your children, not throw them away like so much rubbish when they have problems, and for certain if you were so sure your son was as bad into drugs as you claim, I as a father myself would have been moving heaven and earth to ensure my and your granddaughter was safe; in this case it's obvious you are just trying to use what is your son's illness to your own advantage; we have years of reports from Substance Abuse clinics in the City which not only prove your son has taken full responsibility for his own problems but has been clean for years; your actions are shameful".

As for me, it had been proven by extensive search of my medical records that while I had depression I had never been locked up, in fact it highlighted the attendance I had made to our local Mental Health Hospital where I had been told in no uncertain terms there was nothing wrong with me, but the psychiatrist very much wanted to see my husband.

So, his scheming had sealed his fate.

With his usual 'I am right, I am God, you will conform' ways, his demeanour in Court was to confront the judge trying the case, telling the judge he was wrong and really showing his true colours. To such an extent the Judge told my husband's solicitor he had thirty seconds to inform his client, my husband, the way the courts worked, or he would be held in contempt of court.

When the Court resumed, my husband was told he did not qualify for parental control as only a parent of a child or someone responsible for raising that child got parental control, and as the judge told my husband, "even if you did qualify you would not get parental control, you certainly do not deserve it". The judge also told my husband "it's blatantly obvious you have lied to everyone concerning your own children, their way of life and their natures; while your son had dabbled in drugs he was man enough to admit it and seek help; your daughter is a credit to society thanks mainly to her mum's, your wife's, influence. I'm also awarding full parental responsibility and a full residence order to your wife".

My husband was absolutely furious. We could hear him shouting and yelling at his solicitor as we left the courts.

His solicitor sure earned his money that day.

During all this emotional upheaval I had to take time off from the store, which really did not go down well at all.

My health suffered massively, but my grandchild was glad she did not have to see her grandfather again. I told her if she wanted to visit him at any point, I would let her, but it had to be her choice.

But now that all the commotion began to settle, I noticed changes in her behaviour. At school she was doing very well but socially she suffered. I asked her school to monitor her and because of what we had all gone through in the last few years I put her into school counselling sessions to try and help her understand her life and what had been happening with her grandfather.

Her mother had not only given her away at an incredibly young age, but her half-sister, who is some six years older than my granddaughter, also had been given away by her mother at a similar age to my grandchild.

All this was bound to impact a young impressionable child. This is when my granddaughter started to self-harm. She just could not process all her life events and my husband's behaviour certainly had not helped her or any of us.

Once again, I had to ask work for time off, but they would not accommodate me. I asked if I could have a flexi-hours contract, and I was met with a resounding no, yet other employees were being allowed time off for the silliest reasons. That is when I had my second heart attack, once again taking minimal time off to recover due to the pressure the store was putting on me.

I bought the Union in to the store at that point. Our then part-time HR woman told the Union there was no movement within our Store to enable me to have a flexi contract. I had explained to HR about my grandchild's self-harming but there was no compassion for our situation at all. I had to be at home when my grandchild was at home; she had to be watched at all times. At one point my grandchild had barricaded herself in her room, shouting through the door that no one cared about her. We had to take her door off her room at that point. The HR woman even told me to move stores, the nearest one being quite a distance away – not good if I needed to get to my grandchild in an emergency. I explained this situation to the HR woman and her reply was, "well the company have just opened a small store near the edge of the city, go to that store", not "I will help you to get a position at any of these stores" but just leave and go to another store.

The way a member of staff moved stores was to be transferred internally; that option was not given to me, blatantly trying to get rid of me.

I had by now had my grandchild referred to our local Mental Health Service CAMHS who were investigating.

She remained under their care for some years, subsequently getting a diagnosis of Asperger's syndrome and ADHD and in recent years also Border line personality disorder, anxiety, and depression.

The store became so vile to me at this point, it became blatantly obvious I was being railroaded into constructive dismissal. I was only allowed two fifteen-minute breaks in an eight-hour shift, which is illegal.

And pushed from pillar to post more so than was usual in jobs around the store.

The store would employ you in a low paid position then written into your contract it would state they could ask you to do anything within the store within your hours on shift. It also stated to refuse would lead to disciplinary action, so if you refuse you were instantly given a warning. I had seen employees over the years pushed out of their jobs by use of these contracts, they would use this method if they didn't like an employee or, like me, you stood up for yourself, challenging them if you knew they were in the wrong about anything. They really did not like people who stood up to them.

I was terrified of losing my job. I had a young child relying on me as well as her mentally sick dad.

As I was leaving the store one day after my shift, I came through the back exit door on to the shop floor, which was the way we left this store only one entrance and exit for staff in this store.

Someone had dropped grapes just behind the door, not visible from the side I was exiting. There should have been a mat in front of this section to catch loose spilled grapes, but the cleaner that morning had lifted this mat to clean and not replaced it, causing a slip hazard. I was unaware of this danger, it being obscured from my side of the door.

My feet went from under me. I went airborne, coming down on my elbow which I heard snap, and banging my head. I blacked out for a few seconds, coming round to find the first aider over me telling me to stay down. I was taken to hospital where it was diagnosed I had broken the head of my elbow, the ulnar bone, trapping the ulnar nerve; this was fixed in an operation with screws and pins.

I went home to convalesce. I had a slight headache. Two days later I was back in hospital with a brain haemorrhage caused by the same accident and not picked up at the time of my original hospital admission.

This resulted in me being on heparin and, so I am told, a stay in hospital of some days. I do not have any recollection of that period at all from just before my collapse at home, and for some time after my discharge back home again. This resulted in my being off work from the store for over a year. During this period I had to attend hospital for a camera to be inserted up my nose to the back of my eye to monitor the build-up in fluids in my subarachnoid fissure – if this fluid had built up too much causing too much pressure, it had to be drained. This affected my memory in lots of ways, from constantly repeating the same sentence over and over to complete blanks in memory, and to this day I'm still affected by memory issues which vary from day to day.

This also meant it was incredibly hard to help my grandchild with her issues which continued when I attended her CAMHS appointments, which her doctor, aware of my accident, would write down important items for me to refer to at home.

From the time of my accident no one from the store bothered to contact me to see how I was. At that point I had been employed with them some twenty-five years; so much for caring for their staff.

It brought home just how apt that saying is, you are just a number.

After a year I was deemed by my doctors of being capable to return to work, although not in the job I had been doing as I was now classed as disabled – the accident had damaged my Ulnar Nerve leaving me with very little grip in my left hand. I could not lift heavy pots and pans safely; it was too dangerous for me to continue in my previous job role.

The store took this an opportunity to close the staff restaurant for good, meaning all staff now had no means of a hot meal or snack while at work, but this meant once again the present manager, by closing the restaurant, had saved the store a lot of money, making it seem as if he was controlling his budgets well enough to be moved on within the company to a bigger store.

The store put me onto checkouts, which carried its own problems, but by moving to another till rather than the one they had assigned me I managed – this till was the opposite way around, allowing me to manage my disability better.

It did not stop the store from pulling and pushing me around constantly, pulling me off the till to do whatever job they wanted me to do, from shelf stacking, which was incredibly hard with my disability, to fronting up every few minutes which did not need doing, even to directing HGVs to the back door for unloading, which was really hard due to the area and placement of the entrance to the back door entrance, no matter what the weather. I was not provided with all-weather gear while the actual back door staff did have this gear. I was clearly targeted. No other cashier was used and abused in this way.

Before my accident it had been obvious I was being corralled into constructive dismissal. I would have thought that would have changed after my accident but it seems I was wrong. It had not been helped by the fact that the Union had taken the store to tribunal over my accident where it had been proven the store was at fault and I was awarded a large sum of money.

Bearing in mind at that time I had lost a year's wages and had to pay a big solicitor's bill over the children's court case ,which my husband had implemented – this had left me with very little from that award, from which I had purchased my family members a new bed each and a three piece suite, as we had been using garden chairs in our lounge up to that point .

All my household bills, rent etc had been paid during that year off by using my credit cards, which I had to clear from my compensation.

A short while after my return to work, the solicitor who had won my children's court case contacted me to ask if I was now ready to start divorce proceedings against my husband. With hindsight I should have waited, as I really was not fully mentally capable after my brain haemorrhage, but what with everything that had gone on it seemed time to finish things with the man I had married.

The store at this point was really giving me the hardest of times. I was being timed if I asked to go to the loo, at one point even being told to clock in and out for a loo break.

Even though the store was fully aware of my home situation around my granddaughter's self-harming, I was being dragged into the office and threatened with disciplinary procedures if I did not work several late nights a week; no one else had to do that.

It was at this point HR informed me: "why do not you just leave and let us employ someone younger with no underlying health issues?". No mention of the fact that the accident at work had been a cause of a lot of my health issues.

That was when I had my fourth heart attack, subsequently being diagnosed with supraventricular tachycardia, resulting in a heart operation.

My then so-called manager refused to pay me sick pay, telling me I did not qualify for sick pay – this after working for the store for some 26 years. That was it: I tended my resignation, sending Head Office a copy of my resignation letter, spilling the beans on all that had gone on with my situation, resulting in a visit to my home from the Head of HR who promised me she would look into things; but that's as far as that went – after she left I never heard another word from her, but I did get my sick pay.

I contacted the union who said I did have a case for constructive dismissal, but not telling me I only had 30 days to instigate the case, which during those 30 days, the solicitor who had done my child court case contacted me. With my memory issues the Store constructive dismissal case went completely out of my head and by the time I thought about it again some four weeks later, it was over 30 days, too late to action a case. If the Union had told me I only had a 30-day window I would have made a note to remind myself. Once again let down by the system surrounding the store and their back pocket Union, a Union some two years after I started with the store who had taken a massive amount of money from the store to stop employees voting on pay increases. It was now obvious that it also meant this Union would only do so much for an employee, not progressing any cases in which the store would be seen in a bad light.

The solicitor had done a really good job on the child's case but she did not do the same on the Divorce. My case was given to one of their female solicitors who left the company halfway through my case. I was then given another female solicitor who never listened to a word I said, to such an extent that I took my friend with me on the next appointment, stating to my friend "come with me, this woman's not listening to me, she's ignoring my points and what I'm telling her".

Even with this back-up this female solicitor did not seem to comprehend what I wanted and what had gone on during the marriage. The previous solicitor had told me my compensation would not be taken into account as a marital asset as it had happened some six years after leaving my husband, but this new solicitor was telling me it would be taken as part of the marital assets. I told her this man has been living in the marital property for six years rent-free, a property I had paid for, but she told me it did not matter.

She also told me I would have to sell my car and put that money into the pot. I informed her I did not own my car, it was on hire purchase; they even investigated that to see if I was lying, coming back to me saying yes, it is on hire purchase. No mention of the fact that his car was bought and paid for. All during my marriage I had paid all the bills while he put his money away as he said then for our old age – that never happened.

No mention of the company share money I had saved all through our marriage and put into the property, only to ask me if I could prove what I was saying, to which I replied yes, and gave this solicitor all the details; she never even put that to his solicitor.

I even put a letter of complaint in to the head of the company who invited me in for a meeting, telling me this solicitor seemed to have a good handle on my case. What you have to remember is as a layperson you believe the solicitors you are employing are right, especially when you have had a brain injury causing you to not be able to grasp things the way you normally would.

This solicitor then proceeded to inform me I should settle as my husband had kept me by now tied up in court for some ten years with one case and another – her words to me were there will be nothing left of this property for either party to have; it will all go in legal bills.

Her advice to me was "let him keep the property but tell him he must make a will leaving the property when he dies to your grandchild". At that point we only had the one grandchild. "Because if it goes to court it will cost you four thousand pounds just to go to court, at which point the court will order the sale of the property, and after legal bills are taken you will both be left with nothing." When a solicitor, someone with as you believe knowledge of the legal system and legal experience, tells you something like that, you believe them.

Especially when you are not fully compos mentis.

So that is what happened. After a marriage lasting twenty-eight frightening, violent years, I was left with nothing.

Now when I look back, in a lot of ways it stopped my ex-husband from harassing me. With hindsight it was all he ever wanted. He never wanted to be home with his family and when he was he was vile to his family, never going to one single school event, never praising his children when they had achievements, when they were in trouble telling me "they're your kids, you sort out the issue". As if he had not taken any part in creating his children. Love truly is blind. Then after you realise you're in a horrible situation it is too late, you are in a vicious circle that takes you years to escape.

I now have my own home, which I am buying with my son, mainly because both my son and granddaughter have lifelong Mental Health issues. This house is an ex-council property which took me eight long years of being on a Council waiting list to obtain, after leaving my husband. I initially rented this property, but now having some health conditions as well as my disability, I had enquired what would happen to my family when I died, only to be told they would have to move. This is their home and what money I had managed to save over the years I had spent getting this home to a reasonable living standard, so I was appalled that the Council would make them move from this home.

It was pure luck some four years ago that the Government made a new offer around people like me on Pension or Benefits, to buy their Council properties, so I applied and was lucky enough to be given a massive discount, enabling us to obtain a mortgage on this home.

So, I can rest easy when I pass, knowing not only my son and older granddaughter will still have a home, but my share is willed to my younger granddaughter so she will have some sort of inheritance.

Although I have now been on my own some sixteen years, I am very lonely in a lot of ways, but at least I do not have to cower in fear twenty-four hours a day, 365 days a year.

When I consider what I have achieved in those sixteen years, it makes me realise just how much I could have done in my life if I had not been an abused, terrified woman.

My advice to any woman is: if you are in an abusive relationship these days, do not be scared, just walk away.

Life is way too short to live like that; you can work wonders if you are allowed to and have the inner strength.

I sit here writing this, looking around my home, I have a car I bought and paid for outside, I can go on holiday wherever and whenever I want to; admittedly I am not rich, but I manage.

The best thing is I am Free.

I wish with all my heart I had not stayed in that abusive marriage as long as I did, but in those days there was not the help for women that there is now to enable a woman to escape. Indeed so-called professionals made a woman's situation worse by insisting she stayed in a marriage for the sake of the children, stating your children can be taken from you and put in a home. Women in those days were deemed not capable of caring for their children after escaping a doomed marriage, which as in this more enlightened day we now know is really not the case. Women really are the strongest breed.

Through a lot of my married years while working at the store I was too scared to challenge the store's hierarchy, perceiving them to be as abusive and manipulative as my husband. That still is true of the store today, although not as obvious as it was some thirty years ago.

And with all the goings on, the sex, the drugs, the armed robberies among the bread rolls, you really did not know who to trust. It was that old saying, one of many, if your face fits your in, it's not what you know but who, and the classic if you're over 30 years old, you're, as I was told, too old to take things on board as much as a younger person would.

These days young women seem to be able to challenge more around their lives, getting more help with situations than in my younger day.

But after bumping into an ex-work mate from the store just yesterday, I know for a fact the store is still practising their 'if you will not do it you're out' policy – as this lady told me, she has never had to work so hard in the twenty years she has been at the store.

The store has just renamed this particular branch, meaning it's now run on a very tight reign; as my ex-work mate said, "we all now have to do ten jobs for one wage, even down to cleaning toilets".

They have got rid of cleaners, cash offices, price integrity to name just a few departments and associated staff, it's that old if you will not do it you're disciplined and you are out of a job.

So, while I am not employed any more, I am now at a stage where I have my pension so I will manage.

And no abusive man or managers to tell me what I can or cannot do at last, age seventy I finally have some sort of calm in my life albeit a lonely one – I just cannot trust another man, ever.

And as far as my work environment went, well as I have said, if your face fits you're in. I recommend anyone who is contemplating a job in retail, do not do it – not only is there a culture of discrimination, racial slurs, victimisation and downright bullying; on top of that with all the drug taking, stealing and sexual high jinks going on, literally among those bread rolls, as well as the cannabis baked into those bread rolls, it may as well have been easier to have gone on the road with a heavy metal rock and roll band... in a lot of ways the lifestyle is exactly the same.